FIRST STEPS TO CHORAL MUSIC

by

ARCHIE N. JONES

LOIS RHEA

RAYMOND RHEA

$4.00
(In U.S.A.)

BOURNE INC.
Music Publishers
136 WEST 52nd STREET • NEW YORK 19, N. Y.

TABLE OF CONTENTS

The approach to First Steps to Choral Music is based on the assumption that everyone can and should learn to sing. Unlike instrumental music, choral music is based on the fact that each singer has his own instrument and that he is much more independent of the teacher, or of teaching, than is the instrumentalist. Instructions for the singer are therefore, in the present volume, intended to keep teaching techniques at a minimum. The services of the teacher cannot be omitted, of course, and the success of any program must be the combination of the efforts of the singers and the teacher, or conductor, both parties constantly listening, making corrections, retrials, and re-examinations of sounds and effect.

Two basic pieces of equipment are desirable: a piano (or pitch pipe) and a tape recorder. The piano should be used constantly to test the pitch, and as an accompanying instrument when the music contains an accompaniment; never merely to duplicate the harmony of the voice parts, since the piano has a percussive effect and the singer uses, for the most part, sustained tones. The tape recorder is essential in order that both singers and conductor may hear the results of their efforts. Improvements in tone quality will be evident only in proportion to the degree with which the singers can hear their mistakes and therefore correct them.

Although the present volume is intended to be of help to beginning choirs, the material included will be found to be of interest and of musical value for program purposes to choirs of more advanced skill.

Technical descriptions have been kept to a minimum, for the reason that the authors believe that it is not necessary in all cases for the singer to know why; it is sufficient in most cases that he know how.* For the singer to have to learn the exact construction of the parts of the singing apparatus, for example, would confuse him without helping in the slightest degree to form a correct tone, and to sing musically. When a presentation of technical information seems desirable, the teacher may use his or her judgment as to how much, and as to the method of presentation.

Most of the materials presented here are in harmony, because of the belief that intonation and tonality must be learned from the beginning and cannot be superimposed as a skill after the acquisition of tone. Furthermore, the authors firmly believe that all of the elements of choral singing must be developed concurrently, and in this respect, of course, the teacher plays a major role and should not hesitate to refer to lesson numbers out of sequence.

Purposely, in the title and elsewhere, the term "a cappella" will be avoided, since this term refers to a style of musical composition, the kind of music sung by the sixteenth and seventeenth century chapel choirs, the choir furnishing its own accompaniment. In modern times, it has been construed as "unaccompanied" singing. School choirs, however, should sing all types of music in order to acquire the maximum in musical experiences and for better programming.

Although this volume concerns itself largely with vocal techniques during the chorus rehearsal period, it must be remembered that, like other school studies, much depends upon homework. A few minutes of individual practice at home or elsewhere, several times a day, will do as much or more to build the choir as will the rehearsals or practice in groups. It must be remembered also, that no choir is stronger or better than its poorest singer, and therefore *every* member should practice vocally at every possible opportunity.

It is recommended that while the study of voice and vocal problems should be pursued daily, the choir should also rehearse the songs daily, thereby increasing reading ability and, at the same time, preparing a program. Reference should be made constantly from the problems arising in the songs, to the instructions appearing in the early lessons.

The choral material contained herein is intended to constitute two complete programs and includes compositions for girls' and boys' voices in unison and combination and for the girls and boys together.

---

*The teacher will find helpful suggestions in *Techniques in Choral Conducting,* by Archie N. Jones, published by Carl Fischer, Inc.

Posture

Since most rehearsing is done in a seated position, correct sitting posture becomes all important. When the posture is correct, breathing constitutes no problem, the singer being cautioned to make a habit of taking more breath than is needed. The singer will do well to copy the posture of the violinist in the symphony orchestra: sit about halfway forward on the chair, body erect but not stiff, left foot flat on the floor with the upper and lower limbs describing a right angle, the right foot at the side of the right front leg of the chair.

The really important thing about posture is to be sure that the ribs are well above the diaphragm, allowing the latter to expand and contract freely. Check the position of the diaphragm by placing the fingers just below the juncture of the right and left ribs—if the "hollow" is as large as possible and relaxed (loose), the posture is correct. Be sure to "sit up" while singing; never "sit down."

The singing apparatus includes a "tube," comparable, for descriptive purposes, to a rubber water hose. If the hose is bent, or "kinked," the water flow will be diminished, and if bent double, will cease entirely. This fact shows us that the "tube" must be kept open, or straight, to let the tone flow smoothly at all times. To approximate the proper position, clasp the hands behind the head and pull slightly forward. This means that the head must be erect, and the back of the neck arched slightly forward. For an example in nature of this posture, let us take a look at the way the rooster crows. Observe that the rooster in crowing arches his neck in a different position than in normal carriage. The purpose of this "arching" of course is to release the larynx from constriction, or pressure, in order to let the tone flow smoothly through it. The throat is never used in singing—tone merely passes through it.

In addition to the rooster, three other animals might well be mentioned with regard to singing, because of the lessons they can teach us. To emphasize the importance of opening the mouth (dropping the jaw), let's take a look at the crocodile. A good tone must have a good mouth opening. The pig is a master of diaphragmatic action beginning each grunt from the diaphragm, and the cow, of course, a master of resonance, each "moo" a beautiful example of complete "resounding."

Posture in standing is fundamentally the same as when seated. Stand erect, with one foot slightly advanced (not more than two inches), the weight resting on the forward foot, the toes at a slight outward angle. The chest should be high, to keep the upper part of the body off the diaphragm, shoulders in a natural position, and the neck arched slightly.

Relaxation is the keynote in correct posture. Relaxation may be defined as "freedom from tension." When any of the parts of the body used in singing are tense, bad tone always results. Especially is this true of the throat muscles and larynx (a cartilage within the throat which contains the vocal cords). These must be free and loose at all times. If the throat is tight, the resulting tone will include an unpleasant tremolo or vibrato (shaking). While a natural vibrato is desirable, it should be allowed to develop gradually and naturally from an ever increasing resonance and proper throat action. Do *not* try to force a vibrato in the tone. Here again, relaxation will be helpful. Tension sets up a physical resistance, which in turn affects the tone, especially in loud singing; therefore the singer is urged, particularly in the beginning stages, not to try to sing loudly.

Although it is possible to practice posture, such practice would of necessity consist in assuming correct posture, standing and seated. No posture exercises, therefore, are included. The singer must *remember* to assume the correct posture *before* starting a tone. Remember also that all postures must be natural; the body cannot function properly in unnatural positions.

A good posture "exercise" is always (when singing) to look self-confident. This is a matter of stage presence, and usually results in a correct singing posture. Watching oneself in a full length mirror is helpful in this respect.

LESSON II

Breathing

An excellent little volume entitled "Why Breathe?"[1] is available to teachers and students who believe that breathing is all-important. The author states that athletes and singers made their reputations by "discovering new heights and depths" of breath control. This means merely that people who use the breath as an essential part of the technique of doing something else, must take more breath than in normal breathing and use it with better control. Good breathing should be developed concurrently with the other singing techniques.

Rather than to use specific exercises for improvement in breathing, it is the *constant* application of a few simple but fundamental rules applied to the singing of every phrase:

1. Always breathe deeply;

2. Always take more breath than is needed;

3. Always inhale quickly;

4. Always control the exhalation or expulsion of breath;

5. Sing phrases of constantly increasing length.

Be sure that no breath escapes between the vocal cords without being used in the making of the tone, since this results in a "breathy" tone.

The diaphragm is the control center of breathing. It lies at the base of the lungs in the shape of a saucer, upside down. When a breath is being inhaled, the diaphragm moves downward, and the ribs move outward. When the singer is "full" of breath, the diaphragm and ribs are expanded to capacity, the lungs are full, and the diaphragm "takes over" from here on. Until the next inhalation, the diaphragm controls the tone. Breath control is largely a matter of conserving the breath, and expelling it in such a way that it is used to maximum capacity in the production of the tone. No singer must ever be quite "out of breath," because tones sung without breath support lack vitality and fullness.

Sing Exercises 1 and 3 several times, in Exercise 3 each singer breathing at different places. This is called "staggered" breathing and is done so that the tone of the ensemble goes on without break. The exercises may be sung in unison by each part and then in harmony, using as many parts as desirable. For pronunciataion of the Italian vowels, see Lesson VI.

---

[1]Kellog, Irwin, "Why Breathe?", New York, G. Schirmer, Inc., 1939, 62 pages.

LESSON III

Tone

Although more than ninety per cent of the singing tone is sustained on vowels, it is more often than not started on a consonant, and, therefore, the first consonant of each word becomes very important. For convenience, consonants are classified as vocal or pitch consonants (*m, n, ng, l, v,* and *z*), partial pitch (*d, g*); and non-pitch or surds (*t, h, s, f, p, sh,* and others). We refer to the pitch consonants as such because pitch or vocal tone may be sustained in the consonant; to partial pitch consonants as such because while pitch may reside in the consonant, it cannot be sustained; and to non-pitch consonants because they are incapable of vocal pitch. A consonant which is produced by "hissing" is called a sibilant, but all sibilants are classed as surds, since they, too, may not be sung.

Since the vowel is more easily "exploded" from a "humming" consonant, we will begin the tones in the first few exercises from the consonants *m* and *l*. It is good practice to start the *m* with an *h* in order to connect the breath properly (*hm*).

To approximate the correct mouth position (for all open vowels), place two fingers, one on top of the other, in the mouth. Always refer to opening the mouth as "dropping the jaw," since this implies a relaxed or loose jaw, and this is extremely important. This mouth position must be made a habit; it must become automatic. The tongue should be "out of the way," but if this becomes a conscious action, it may result in tone blocking. Try to forget the tongue; just keep it from interfering with the tone. Use a mirror to see whether or not the mouth is open and the jaw down, and try each time the mouth is opened for a tone to approximate the same position.

We are now ready to produce the tone. In Exercise 1, before singing, count the rhythm aloud in class, in order that when singing, the singers may concentrate entirely on the sound of the tone. Since the vowel *ah* suggests the best mouth position, and the consonant *hm,* the best resonance, we will begin the tone with "hm," opening into the "ah" after about two seconds (or at the beginning of the second beat), and continuing the exercise on the vowel. Repeat the exercise in keys successive half steps higher and lower.

The singer should try constantly to remember that all singing tone is a matter first of mental concept. Good tones don't just happen, at least very often . . . they are planned in the mind; at first, each one is planned separately; then as singing becomes a habit, good tones become automatic. It should be remembered, however, that for the first few months no tone should be started until the singer is fairly certain that the sound which comes from the throat will at least approximate the sound which his mind has first "imagined."

We are now ready for our first song, "Pledge of Allegiance." Note first that the unit of beat is the quarter note. Count the rhythm first: 4-1-2-3-4, 1-2-3, then breathe, and continue. Watch for breathing places, usually where there is a comma, but not always. Then speak the words aloud together. This will make the pitch and harmony easier. Now sing the first phrase, concentrating on tone. Be sure all are satisfied with the quality and quantity of tone before continuing. Great care must be exercised in order to keep the quality of tone standard (the same for each word). When in doubt, return to Exercise 1, to test the tone.

Student Conductors:

In order that the teacher may use his full time in the supervision of tone, and since the class must sing the exercise in exact rhythm, it is wise to use a system of student conductors to keep the class together. This technique, in addition, gives conducting experience to the students. This experience will be valuable in the future programs of the choir.

It is wise to ask the singers to take turns in conducting in order that each may have the experience and in order that one, or a few, will not miss too much of the vocal practice. The standard beat outlines are included here for convenience:

TWO-FOUR METER:

THREE-FOUR METER

FOUR-FOUR METER

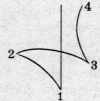

SIX-EIGHT METER

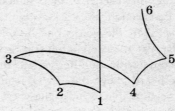

EXERCISE 1

For breathing and humming

Hm-ah. _____

LESSON IV

Blend

One of the factors in tone is the *blend* of the voices. In the building of a chorus or choir, it is necessary to be certain that no one or more voices "stick out." If one voice is heard above all other voices, either it is because that voice is too loud or is not producing the same color of tone.

Color is different in various voices because of the presence or absence of overtones and because of the degree to which these are present or absent. For convenience, voices are classified as light, medium, and dark. Each voice (on the professional level) should be able to sing all three colors, as the mood of the music indicates. Since most choruses and choirs are too light in color, it is wise to try to "darken" the color, on the assumption that they will eventually become "medium," which is the ideal color.

In blending the voices, the class should begin with the soprano part of Exercise 1. After all have sung, the teacher or class should choose the voice which represents the best in tone quality in that section; then ask every other soprano to pattern her tones in Exercise 1 on the chosen tone. Add the voices one by one, until all of the sopranos have sung the exercise together. Repeat the exercise several times in order to make the tone color a habit. Use the same procedure with the alto section, then the tenor, and finally the bass. If certain voices can still be heard above the others, it means either that they are singing too loudly or that they have been unable to make the vocal adjustments necessary to produce the desired color. The volume from all voices should be the same: in other words, the entire section should sound as one voice. In case a particular singer finds it impossible to blend with the others, in extreme cases it may be necessary to ask the singer to study privately with a voice teacher until he is able to control the tone.

After the singers are blended in their respective sections, it is then necessary to follow the same procedure by *sections* rather than with individual singers in blending the entire chorus. No section should be heard above another, and all should sing approximately the same color. Exercise 2 will be helpful in enabling the singers to listen to and correct the blend.

As in the string section of the symphony orchestra, choir tone depends upon the color of the voices and the differences in the speed of the various vibratos. Wide vibratos are unpleasant and usually due to too much "pressure" on the larynx, or throat. These can be reduced by throat relaxation. Within limits, variations in vibrato speed are desirable. However, if one voice "sticks out" because of too wide or prominent a vibrato, this voice should have individual training until the vibrato can be controlled.

Voices without vibrato also are welcome in the choir, since this adds to the "smoothness" of tone. In no case should a vibrato be attempted if it is not present. The vibrato will come naturally with the training of the voice.

"The Lord is My Shepherd" for girls' voices has been chosen because of the necessity for perfect blend in singing it! Sing over the first phrase slowly, establishing the blend as outlined for Exercise 1, gradually increasing the tempo until the desired speed is attained, but remembering always to sing good tones with a perfect blend. Remember, too, that blend depends upon *listening to each other*.

After the girls have learned to blend their voices together, the boys should sing the baritone part of "Beautiful Saviour." When the boys have achieved a good blend, sing all three parts together, first without accompaniment so that each singer can hear the others. Refer to the blending exercises (1 and 3) frequently.

Balance

After the blend has been established, it is necessary next to establish a proper balance. An equal volume of sound should come from all the parts.

One method of establishing balance is to ask the sopranos and altos to sing Exercise 2, the tenors and basses listening. It will be obvious which part is louder than the other or if both sopranos and altos sound with equal balance. If one part is louder than another, more voices should be added to the weaker part or subtracted from the stronger. Shifting of voices from one part to another is permissible, providing the voice range is easy in the new part.

After the sopranos and altos are balanced, the sopranos and basses may listen to the altos and tenors, repeating the procedures outlined above. Then the sopranos and altos may listen to the tenors and basses. Finally, the teacher listens to the choir as a whole. It usually is found that a few more voices are necessary in the alto and bass sections than in the soprano and tenor, since the high voices sound louder than the low voices.

Balance cannot be tested at one level of loudness or softness alone. It is necessary (not in the individual sections, but in the choir as a whole) to sing pianissimo, mezzo forte, and fortissimo, in order to establish the proper balance for each. Sing Exercise 1 at all three levels and test the balance at each level. Use crescendo and decrescendo (see glossary of musical terms) frequently. The ears of the singers constitute the best test, and each singer should be cautioned never to sing so loudly that he can hear his own voice above the others in his section.

After testing the balance, using Exercise 1, sing through the first two phrases of "Beautiful Savior," using the same techniques, each singer constantly listening to the other parts and never allowing his or her voice to become more audible than the others. Success in balance is attained by subduing one's own voice for the good of the entire ensemble.

In order to establish the balance for four part harmony, sing "Now Thank We All Our God," and "All Things Are Thine."

EXERCISE 2

Balance and blend (Sustain each voice until all voices blend as one, then add next voice). Stagger the breathing. Use all Italian vowels on these two exercises.

LESSON VI

The Vowels

People often wonder why we use the Italian language so much in singing practice. There are several reasons, but the most important one is very simple. The Italian language contains only "pure" vowels, that is, vowels which make only one sound. English, on the other hand, has many diphthongs, or combinations of vowel sounds, which are unpleasant in singing. For example, in the English word "sky," we pronounce it "skah-ee," which sounds unpleasant in singing unless the final "ee" is tacked on at the very end of the sound. To make the proper vowel sounds into habits, therefore, we use the Italian vowels, the pronunciations of which are approximately as follows:

a—ah

e—ay (without the final "y" sound)

i—ee

o—oh

u—oo

One of the favorite exercises (vocalises) in many systems of singing, attaches a singing or pitch consonant to the vowels in the following manner:

"lah-bay-dah-may-nee-poh-too"

This vowel sequence will be found to be very helpful in establishing the habit of always singing the same vowel shapes. Use Exercise I with each vowel throughout the exercise, changing keys progressively one-half step higher for each vowel. Then sing Exercise 2 as indicated, then Exercise 3, 4, and 6. Remember to use Italian pronunciation for all vowels.

We begin with the vowel "ah" since it represents the most natural mouth position, and the one most easily habituated. Remember to drop the jaw to the extent that the mouth is at least "two fingers" open. Try this vowel formation in front of a mirror, and for the first few times ask the teacher to correct the mouth position for each vowel.

To describe the mouth positions for the various vowels is very difficult. However, a brief description is here attempted as an aid to proper mouth positions. The teacher should check each singer's position frequently. One of the major purposes of voice study is *vowel equalization,* which means singing each vowel so that all tones sound the same, regardless of which vowel is sung. The tones of a French horn, for example, are the same throughout the easy register. With the voice, two problems make keeping the tone the same much more difficult; first, the vocal tone is much more easily distorted in singing the various parts of the range than is true of an instrument, and, second, the mouth must assume several different shapes in producing the various vowels.

In general, there are two fundamental lip and teeth positions: (1) open, and (2) almost closed. The latter position is used only for the vowels *ee* and *oo*. The *oo* sound (as in "boot") is made with the lips in a "blowing" position, with the tongue slightly lower than, and slightly forward of center. As the pitch rises, it will be necessary to open the lips and teeth slightly and inject a very little of the "oh" sound, especially in the very high notes.

In "planning" the vowel sounds, it is a good idea to whisper the vowels before singing them, using a mirror to check the shapes. This can be done at home, and should be practiced several days in succession while the classwork is concerned with vowel study.

The "ee" sound is made from the "oo" position, keeping the lips and teeth almost the same as in "oo," but lowering the tongue so that the tip rests lightly against the lower teeth and relaxing the lips very slightly.

To make the "oh" sound, sing "ah," then make the mouth and lip position a little rounder, closing the teeth very slightly and keeping the tongue in the same position. Be careful not to close the mouth more than slightly or the "oh" will sound muffled.

The "ay" sound is also made from "ah," widening slightly the mouth and teeth and raising the tongue slightly and pushing it forward, and at the same time arching the hard palate slightly higher. Here again care must be taken not to overdo it, remembering that the whole purpose is to make the tone sound the same for all vowels.

Perhaps the most difficult vowel in English is the short "i," as in the word "blink." Probably the best way to approach this vowel is from the sound "uh," which is made with the mouth open slightly "taller" than "ah." To sing short "i," sing "uh," then close the mouth position very slightly, raising the tongue a little, being careful to use more resonance.

For practice in the proper singing of all of the vowels, use Exercise 1 again, starting each vowel with "hm," which, it will be remembered, is used to establish resonance.

It must be remembered that in singing the exercises, the Italian vowels are used; when singing the songs, of course, the English vowels are used, but the singers are cautioned in singing diphthong vowels ("a" as in "lake," "i" as in "sky," "o" as in "home") to place the final vowel at the very end of the sound. Example: "leh----eek" $=$ "lake."

Worthy of mention is the little downward projection in the upper back of the throat called the *uvula*. For "ah;" "uh," and "ih," the uvula is in a relaxed position; pay no attention to it. For "ee," "oo," "oh," and "ay," it should be held rather high, as in a yawn.

Sing Exercise 3 slowly, paying particular attention to vowel pronunciation, making sure that the closing of diphthongs are sung quickly and smoothly.

"My House of Life" represents a good example of the use of vowels, since almost all of the vowels are represented within each phrase. Sing the entire song slowly, giving each vowel plenty of time in formation, but do not exaggerate. Keep the mouth open "tall," rather than "wide," except for the vowels *ee* and *oo,* and be sure to give these plenty of resonance.

Exercise 4 attaches certain consonants to the Italian vowels. Sing the exercise through, taking a breath at the end of the second measure, taking care that the consonant "opens" into the vowel.

EXERCISE 3

Breathing (Italian vowels). Stagger the breath and sing whole exercise without break in tone.

I, e, a, o, u, o, u, ah. _____

EXERCISE 4

For emphasizing consonants (also Italian vowels)

La, be, de, mo, ni,_ po,_ tu, ca, re, se, te, mi, re, le.

LESSON VII

Resonance

All perfect tones must have resonance; in other words, they must resound (re-sound). Nature has provided most voices with perfect resonators. However, it takes a great deal of practice to use them properly in singing. Tones produced in the front part of the mouth only lack resonance. In fact that part of the mouth is used for the purpose of pronouncing the words. Good resonance comes from the back part of the mouth and the nasal cavities of the head. Without resonance, the tone lacks carrying quality and virility.

To establish resonance (remember that this is partially the purpose of Exercise 1), use lots of humming, and when opening from the consonant into the vowel, try to keep the same quality in the tone, avoiding purely nasal sounds. Place the fingers lightly on the upper chest to test the resonance. If a slight vibration is felt, and the listeners report a pleasant sound, the chances are that there is some resonance present. The teacher should check the resonance with each singer, and the singers should listen to each other by individuals and by sections. Try speaking dramatically (stage lines), using a vibrant quality but not too loud. Try to keep this quality in the singing tones.

The tone which best approximates the singing tone with regard to resonance is the tone of the cello. The resonance cavities of the head are somewhat like the resonance of the cello. One of the purposes of resonance is that of reinforcing the overtones. To acquire an idea of how important this principle is in singing, a demonstration may be provided in a simple way. The pianist may hold down the damper pedal and the fingers on the keys in a C Major chord, without sounding them. One of the tenors with a resonant voice should then sing close to the strings of the piano (beneath the raised lid of a grand piano) a flat, short "a" sound (a sound rarely used in singing because of its lack of resonance) on the pitch middle "C", allowing time for the class to hear the sound in the piano. Then sing a resonant "oo" and "oh," noting the differences in the sounds from the piano strings and sounding board. Try all the vowels in the same manner. It will be noted that the strings "pick up" the overtones by the means of sympathetic vibrations, and the ear quickly hears which vowels need resonance reinforcement.

Go back to Exercise 1, and instead of allowing the tone to open into the vowel, sing the chords with a hum. Then repeat the exercise with the vowels, but retaining the hum quality in the vowels. Be very careful to avoid nasal tones. The tone should resound, not allowed to come through the nose.

"O Bone Jesu" is especially well adapted to learning to sing resonant tones. Sing the song slowly, one part at a time (tenors, basses, altos, sopranos, in that order), all sections listening to each other, and adjusting the tones until all are satisfied that the proper degree of resonance is present.

LESSON VIII

Humming

LEGATO AND STACCATO

One of the musical terms used most frequently with regard to singing, is *legato*. Legato means *smooth*. It is contrasted with another musical term *staccato*, meaning disconnected, the opposite of *smooth*. While staccato is used frequently in instrumental music, it is more rarely encountered in vocal music.

One of the best methods of achieving a legato tone is through the technique of humming. Several methods of humming are in general use, but the one preferred by most conductors is produced by singing the vowel "uh," then almost closing the jaw, but not the teeth, and leaving the lips very slightly parted, just enough so that a slight vibration is felt while humming. In this way, there is created not only a pleasant tone, but one which is capable of making both loud and soft tones.

If the hum is made continuous, it is impossible, of course, to achieve anything but a *legato*. Begin with Exercise I, continuing the hum throughout the exercise, and observing a crescendo and decrescendo. The attack for the hum should be started with an "h."

Since most humming choruses are written and intended to be sung without phrasing, it is necessary to use "staggered breathing." This means that only a few singers can breath at any one time. If all of the singers will avoid taking breaths in expected places, this will usually work itself out without practice, but if, after the first time through a chorus or exercise, it develops that there are "holes" in the humming, or places where the breathing is noticeable, it will be necessary to "plan" the breathing. This can be done by numbering the singers within each part, and numbering the measures within the song, and assigning breaths to the singers by number. In this way, only so many singers will take a breath in each breathing place and a continuous *legato* will be assured.

The humming song "Pastorale," is an excellent example of music without words. Sung with a *legato,* and with as wide a range of dynamics as the humming will allow, the humming song makes an excellent program piece, enjoyable for both singers and audience. It cannot, of course, be overdone. More than one on a program would be monotonous.

The Chorales constitute excellent humming pieces also. It is good practice to hum these with and without phrasing, in either case varying the dynamics as the music indicates.

Although *staccato* is encountered infrequently in singing, it is sometimes used and, therefore, some practice would be valuable. Exercise 5 is intended to emphasize staccato, pitch, and diction. Sing the exercise first very slowly, increasing the tempo with each repetition. Be very careful to sing each tone on the exact pitch. Singing too loudly will result in singing off pitch. Sing the first note rather loudly and then repeat it softly, at the same time looking at the *next* note, so that the pitch concept will be mental as well as physical.

Next, sing the chorale "Now Thank We All Our God," singing each word *staccato,* again being careful to start and end each tone on the exact pitch, always looking ahead to see what the pitch of the next note is.

Exercise 5 is a study in staccato and legato, again using the Italian vowels. Sing it first *staccato,* being sure that the dynamic level is low enough so that the tones are pleasant. Next, sing the exercise *legato,* but being careful that the tone does not *slur* or *scoop*.

EXERCISE 5

Staccato and legato singing

La, be, de, mo, ni,_ po,_ tu, ca, re, se, te, mi, re, le.

La, be, de, mo, ni,_ po,_ tu, ca, re, se, te, mi, re, le.

La, be, de, mo, ni, po, tu, ca, re, se, te, mi, re, le.

La, be, de, mo, ni, po, tu, ca, re, se, te, mi, re, le.

LESSON IX

Attack and Release

Since all tones must be made first in the mind, probably the most important part of a tone is its beginning, or *attack*. Several words of caution are necessary. First, the attack must be made on the exact pitch indicated; second, it must be made on time; third, it must be made at the proper dynamic level; and fourth, the diction must be clear. Attacks on consonants and vowels are made in different ways.

Consonants:

For singing, or pitch consonants, a slight degree of exaggeration is valuable. For example, in Exercise 3, hold the "singing consonants" slightly before "exploding" into the vowel. The singing, or pitch consonants in the exercise are l, m, n, and r. While holding the consonant, think how the following vowel should sound, and then gently open into the vowel. The singers should check each other in this exercise, criticising each sound and the sounds of the various parts. Do the exercise first with *staccato,* concentrating on the attack, which should be done mezzo forte.

For half-pitch consonants (b, d, g), not so much exaggeration is desirable, but just enough to establish the pitch. The nonpitch consonants (t, p, f, s, etc.), should be produced without emphasis, and left as quickly as possible. Avoid at all times the "stroke of the glottis," in which the uvula strikes the palate with an explosive sound. The uvula should always stroke the palate gently, never explosively.

Vowels:

Attacks on vowels are much more difficult tonally than on consonants, until the singer has learned to make all vowels sound approximately the same. Generally, it may be said that all vowels begin with an aspiration, or an "h" sound. The "h" is almost inaudible, but is present nevertheless. Sing Exercise 4 first with a breath after each vowel, and beginning each with an "h" sound. Remember to sing the Italian pronunciation. Repeat the exercise until all the singers are attacking each vowel at precisely the same instant. Very few faults annoy an audience so much as ragged attacks. Remember that an attack must be made at the beginning of each phrase, and therefore all the singers must constantly watch the conductor.

Several attack systems are used by various conductors, the bottom of the beat, the delayed beat, an extra motion after the beat, and so on. Generally however, most singers find it easier to make the attack at the exact bottom of the beat. Much practice will make this habitual, and only after it has become habitual will it be precise.

One of the dangers in the attack is the *slur*. The attack must not be "scooped," or slurred, but made exactly on the pitch. The pitch, although indicated by a note sometimes an eighth of an inch wide, is only "pin-point" wide, and this means for all singers and all parts. If a number of the singers have slightly different ideas as to the exact pitch, the harmony will sound "muddy."

The release is also important, and here again releases are different, depending upon whether the release is on a vowel or consonant. If on a vowel, the release usually is made by an aspiration (ending with an "h"), as in the word "you." When the signal for the release is made, the singers should not "stop" the stream of air sustaining the tone, but simply let it slip away by attaching an "h" at the end of the vowel. Care should be taken that the "h" is not audible.

The release of the consonant will vary with the consonant. In general, pitch and half-pitch consonants are concluded with a silent, or almost silent "uh" sound; for example, "them-uh." This amounts only to a slight exaggeration of the final consonant. For the nonpitch consonants, or surds, great care must be taken in the release, especially in the sibilant, or "hissing" consonants. "The Lord of Hosts" is a difficult release unless care is taken not to exaggerate the "ts." If most of the singers will finish the word "Hosts" with a "th" (Hoth), with only one or two designated to pronounce the "ts" clearly, the total effect will be much better than if everyone tries to pronounce the "ts" independently.

Many conductors give too many release signals. These are necessary at the ends of phrases which are not followed in rhythm and tempo, and at the ends of *fermatas,* but otherwise the attacks and releases both should be left to the rhythm of the words. This means, of course, that the singers must become expert in timing.

The attack should be practiced with Exercise 5, attacking each syllable separately, and slowly, being very precise about attacking together, as one voice. This exercise may be used also for vowel release as described above. For consonant release, simply add the various consonants to the syllables of Exercise 5.

Exercise 6 represents a study not only in *staccato* and *legato,* attack and release, but rhythmic precision as well. All voices must sing each syllable at exactly the same time.

"Gloria Patri" shows the necessity for rhythmic precision and emphasizes the delicate balance between staccato and legato. Be sure, when singing this song, that not only do the individual voices sing the syllables of each chord at exactly the same time but that each chord is sung on the exact pitch and all notes appearing before rests released a little before the time indicated by the note values. This will give the singers time for the breath, and enable the next chord to start on time.

Exercise 7, in 6/8 meter, should be used for practice in attack, rhythmic precision, and *staccato* singing. Increase the tempo each time, repeating the exercise several times, at various dynamic levels.

EXERCISE 6

Rhythmic precision

A - long our sing - ing path we go, path we go.

A - long our sing - ing path we go, path we go.

A - long our sing - ing path we go, path we go.

A - long our sing - ing path we go, path we go.

EXERCISE 7

Staccato (emphasizing enunciation and pronunciation). Also Italian vowels

La, be, de, mo, ni, po, tu, la, be, de, mo, ni, po, tu.

La, be, de, mo, ni, po, tu, la, be, de, mo, ni, po, tu.

La, be, de, mo, ni, po, tu, la, be, de, mo, ni, po, tu.

La, be, de, mo, ni, po, tu, la, be, de, mo, ni, po, tu.

LESSON X

Phrasing

To most singers, phrasing is synonymous with breathing, and it is true that the two are related, in that one usually breathes at the end of the phrase. However, this represents only a part of phrasing. The simplest example of musical phrasing is in the *Chorale,* two of which are included in this volume, for the reason that the musical, dramatic, breath, and poem phrases coincide. Generally speaking, the phrasing of a song centers around dynamics. Each succeeding phrase should be slightly louder (unless the context makes it inappropriate) until the climax, and then successively softer. In addition, each phrase should contain a slight crescendo and decrescendo. In outline form this would look as follows for a four phrase song.

An example of the above is "On Wings of Song." Exercise 8 is also planned for phrasing practice. A slight impulse should be made on the word "wings," then a *crescendo* at the beginning of the second full measure, with a decrescendo at the end of the word "fly." The important thing to remember is that the loudest part of the climax *crescendo* must be louder than the loudest part of any of the other *crescendos.*

Sometimes the musical and word phrases will not coincide, although they usually do in well-written music. When they do not, however, the singer must remember to follow the musical phrasing, at the same time being careful not to break up words or word phrases with breaths.

Use the chorales for practice in phrasing, making slight *crescendo-decrescendo* patterns within each phrase. It should be remembered that the time for a breath should always be taken from the word the singer is leaving, not the one he is approaching. In this way, each phrase will begin on time.

In Exercise 9, there should be a slight crescendo in each three-note group and a larger one over the middle of the whole phrase. Remember that phrasing applies to all of the parts, so the tenors and basses must also sing the *crescendo-decrescendo,* in order to maintain the proper balance.

20

EXERCISE 8

The birds the birds are home-ward, home-ward wing-ing.

EXERCISE 9

Italian vowels (also phrasing)

A, e, i, o, u.

LESSON XI

Pianissimo Singing

The safe dynamic level for singing, and consequently the level at which most practice is done, is mezzo forte. When singing becomes too loud, tones are distorted and unpleasant. *Pianissimo,* or very soft singing is much neglected and rarely achieved by most choruses. However, true *pianissimo* is thrilling, both for chorus and audience, although too much of it would, like too much of anything else, become monotonous.

To achieve true pianissimo, much practice is necessary. Begin with Exercise 2, since only the sopranos begin at the beginning, and the other parts can check the softness of tone. Begin again and again until all of the singers are satisfied that the sopranos are singing as softly as they can sing and still sing a good round tone, and then bring in the other parts at no louder a dynamic level. One way to learn to sing softly is to aspirate (after a deep breath), and after a very short time of allowing the "h," or stream of air to escape, attach a very soft tone on a vowel, sustaining it as long as possible.

The "Pastorale" has already been used as a humming song. Repeat this number using the vowel "uh" sung as softly as possible.

Most choirs fail to practice pianissimo, and if they do, fail to apply the practice to the songs they sing. Pianissimo must be practiced constantly, or the choir will find that its dynamic level ranges between *mezzo-forte* and *fortissimo,* instead of from *pianissimo* to *fortissimo.*

Pianissimo phrases may be practiced as excerpts from songs. Such phrases occur in "Gloria Patri" and "I Ain't Gonna Grieve My Lord No More."

Staccato exercises are difficult to sing softly, therefore, they represent excellent studies for this purpose. Sing Exercises 5, 6, and 7, using as soft a tone as possible but not allowing the *vitality* of the tone to be lost.

22

EXERCISE 10

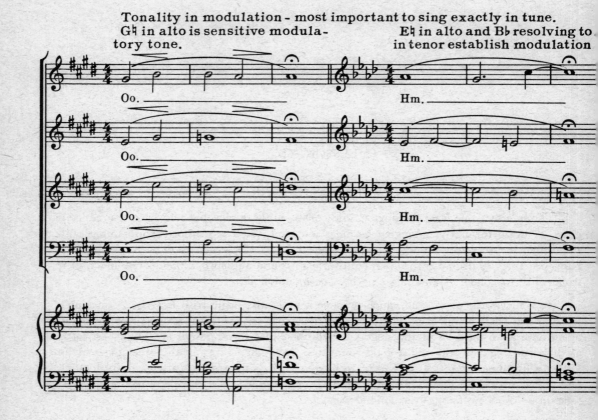

Tonality in modulation - most important to sing exactly in tune.
G♮ in alto is sensitive modula-
tory tone.
E♮ in alto and B♭ resolving to
in tenor establish modulation

LESSON XII

Modulation

Modulation means simply the harmonic progressions necessary in changing keys. Since the vast majority of choruses sing modulations out of tune, failing thereby to establish the new key and losing *tonality,* and since so many choral compositions contain modulations, it seems wise to include exercises and modulatory passages herein.

Several rules are valuable in singing modulations. First, each note within the modulation should be sung in exact pitch; second, the accidentals (flats, sharps and naturals) should be slightly emphasized by the part or parts encountering them; third, when the new key is reached, all parts should slightly emphasize the first few chords. In this way both tonality and intonation may be maintained. If a change of meter is encountered immediately following a modulation, the first few beats of the new meter should be emphasized, and the last few beats of the old meter slightly retarded.

Exercise 10 is intended for practice in modulation. Remember to sing the exact pitches, and emphasize the "natural" signs. Sing the exercise slowly at first, then a little faster each time, but never so fast that the various parts fail to hear the others.

Interpretation

Although interpretation is generally conceived as the conductor's job, nevertheless he finds it impossible without the help of the singers. This is true more of choral music than of instrumental music, since in the former so much depends upon the words.

There are three elements of interpretation; tempo, dynamics, and tone quality. Interpretation is achieved by varying degrees of each, and by following the traditions of style, mood, and context of the words.

Interpretation will not be successful unless the singers feel the words and music. It is therefore necessary to analyze both as the song is rehearsed. When the music is soft, it is soft for a reason; when it is loud, there is always a reason. Singing is physical and emotional, more so than playing an instrument, because the voice is a part of the body. Try to feel each tone, and make the tones express the meaning of the words.

A good technique, when the chorus is having trouble with interpretation, is that of *choral speaking*. Say the words in tempo and rhythm, using inflection instead of pitch, raising the voice when the music is loud or high, and lowering it when it is soft or low. Then sing it through, exaggerating the dynamic levels.

In Lesson III we learned how to make tones dark or light. For interpretive purposes we let the mood of the words guide the color of the tone. Sing through "Prayer" with as dark a tone as possible, using a rather low dynamic level (pianissimo to mezzo-forte). "Ring, Ring the Banjo" may be done with a light tone.

The tempo is usually indicated at the beginning of a song. " =100" means that there should be 100 quarter notes per minute. You can always tell approximately how fast or slow the music should be sung by comparing the metronome indication (= 100) with your pulse which is approximately 80 for boys and approximately 78 for girls. It will be of a great deal of help to the director if each singer tries to feel the correct tempo and keeps it consistently the same.

Each type of composition has its own (approximately) tempo. For example, chorales vary very little in tempo. Sacred compositions are generally quite slow. "The Band Played On" is naturally quite fast, as is "Ring, Ring the Banjo." Oftentimes there will be slow parts and fast parts in the same song, and when this occurs, usually neither the slow or fast parts are extreme.

LESSON XIV

Stage Presence

This title, at first sight, seemingly has little to do with singing; however, either with a soloist, or with the members of a choir it is really very important. With any of the famous choirs, stage presence is a major concern. From the time the choir marches on the stage, until the time of the final chord, the audience is receiving continued impressions which cannot help but influence its reception of the music. Every choir tries to achieve a perfect balance between dignity and vivacity, sincerity and verve, and enthusiasm and restraint.

Marching on stage should be done quickly but with seeming deliberation. Short, quick steps are best, and if there are risers, the steps should be taken at an angle. The robes should be the same distance from the floor; the boys should all wear white shirts and dark ties; and no one feature of clothing of any singer should be conspicuous.

Facial expression is most important. Not only does it affect the vocal tone, but it sets the "tone" of the entire performance. Smile, but do not grin; when the music is serious, the facial expression should be serious. When the music is light, the facial expression should be light. Interest should be registered at all times, and the eyes of all singers should never waiver from the conductor at any time during the singing of a number.

Any motion of any singer is quickly seen by the audience. Hands should be out of sight and motionless. When a number is concluded, everyone should relax, and immediate attention given when the conductor is ready for the next number.

Confidence probably is the keyword in stage presence. If the conductor and every member of the choir is sure of himself, and confident that the concert will be a success, there is no doubt that it will be. On the other hand, the slightest nervousness transmits itself to the audience, and then the choir must prove itself. Confidence is achieved when the choir knows the music, and when the conductor knows what he can expect of the choir. Sincerity is the keynote of confidence. If you are not sincerely interested in singing and in maintaining membership in the choir, go home please!

LESSON XV

Be Sure's

1. Be sure that you understand and apply relaxation—"lack of tension."
2. Be sure always to assume (and sustain) correct posture. Relax it only between songs.
3. Be sure to maintain an even vowel scale. Review Lesson VI.
4. Be sure your jaw is down and relaxed.
5. Be sure you sing the words so they can be "seen."
6. Be sure to take the breath in time (quickly) to attack the next phrase on time.
7. Be sure you are using all your resonance.
8. Be sure you are listening to and can hear the other parts all the time.
9. Be sure that each breath is taken as deeply as possible.
10. Be sure that your voice is no louder or softer than the others.

Beware's

1. Beware of the "breathy" tone.
2. Beware of "oversinging." This comes from overenthusiasm.
3. Beware of slurring. Attack on Pitch.
4. Beware of the sibilant consonants.
5. Beware of the "stroke of the glottis." Make your attacks deliberate.
6. Beware of tremolo or too much vibrato. Don't be a "shaker."
7. Beware of the nasal tone. Anybody can be a newsboy.
8. Beware of "off pitch" singing. A miss is as good as a mile.
9. Beware of the tongue. Don't let it "get in the way."
10. Beware the high notes. Don't distort the quality to achieve the impossible.

GLOSSARY OF MUSICAL TERMS

A Cappella—Vocal music without accompaniment.

A Tempo—In time. Usually a return to the original tempo.

Accelerando—(accel.) Gradually faster.

Accent—Stress or emphasis.

Accidental—A sharp, flat, or natural sign placed before a note to change its pitch.

Adagio—A slow tempo, slower than Andante, not so slow as Lento.

Air—The melody, or tune.

Allegretto—A moderately fast tempo, faster than Moderato, slower than Allegro.

Allegro—A quick, lively tempo, faster than Moderato, slower than Vivace.

Alto—The lowest of the women's voices. Also Contralto.

Andante—A moderately slow tempo, faster than Adagio, slower than Moderato.

Andantino—Slightly faster than Andante.

Animato—Animated, lively.

Anthem—A religious choral composition.

Aria—A solo vocal form, part of an opera or oratorio.

Arpeggio—A broken chord, distinguished from a simultaneous chord.

Art Song—An artistic song in which the music closely fits the words.

Augmented—A term applied to major and perfect intervals enlarged by one-half step.

Ballad—A narrative song.

Barcarolle—A boat song, usually having a smoothly flowing melody.

Baritone—A male voice, between tenor and bass in pitch. Also an instrument.

Bass—The lowest male voice. Also an instrument.

Berceuse—A lullaby, or cradle song.

Cadence—A harmonic ending.

Cantata—A composition with choral and solo parts, built around a central theme.

Carol—A festal folk-song, usually on a Christmas or Easter theme.

Chant—A religious song, with groups of words sung on the same pitch.

Choir—A group of singers, usually for a church service.

Chorale—A hymn-like type of music, usually sacred.

Chord—Three or more tones sounded together harmonically.

Chromatic—Progressing by half-tone intervals.

Coda—An extended ending of a composition.

Coloratura—A specialized type of high soprano voice.

Con fuoco—With fire.

Con moto—With motion.

Consonance—A chord or combination of sounds pleasing to the ear. Opposed to dissonance.

Contralto—The lowest woman's voice. Also alto.

Contrapuntal—Relating to counterpoint.

Counterpoint—The setting of one melody against another.

Crescendo—(cresc.) Increasing in loudness.

Da Capo—(D. C.) To the beginning.

Dal Segno—(D. S.) Literally, from the sign.

Decrescendo—(decresc.) Decreasing in loudness.

Diatonic—Progressing by scale intervals.

Diminished—A term applied to minor and perfect intervals made smaller by one-half step.

Diminuendo—(dim.) Gradually softer.

Dissonance—A combination of sounds unsatisfying to the ear. Opposed to consonance.

Duet—A song for two solo voices or instruments.

Ensemble—Together; a group of players playing together.

Etude—A musical study or exercise.

Fantasia—A free and fanciful form of composition.

Finale—The last part, or close of a composition.

Fine—A term indicating the termination of a composition.

Flat—A symbol (♭) indicating that a tone is to be lowered in pitch one-half step.

Folk-song—A song characteristic of people or nation.

Forte—(f) Loud.

Fortissimo—(ff) Very Loud.

Forzando—(sf) Strongly accented. The same as sforzando (sfz).

Fugue—A common form of contrapuntal composition.

Fundamental—A term applied to the lowest note of a chord in normal position.

Glee—A choral composition for three or four voices.

Grave—A slow and solemn movement. The slowest tempo in music.

Harmonics—Overtones obtained on instruments or voice; usually applied to stringed instruments.

Harmony—Combinations of tones into chords and chordal progressions.

Hymn—A common form of religious song, intended to be sung by the congregation.

Interval—The distance between two tones.

Intonation—The act of production of tone in exact tune or pitch.

Inversion—A change in position from the normal of an interval or chord.

Key—A system of tone relationships following the pattern of a recognized scale.

Largo—A very slow tempo.

Legato—Connected.

Lento—A slow tempo, slower than Adagio, faster than Largo.

Madrigal—A secular part song developed during the sixteenth century.

Maestoso—Majestically.

Major—Greater, when referring to intervals or scales. Opposed to minor.

Marcato—Marked; accented.

Mass—A choral composition performed at the celebration of High Mass.

Measure—The space between two bar lines on the staff.

Melody—A pleasing succession of tones, usually having a pleasing rhythm.

Meno—Less.

Meno mosso—Less motion; slower.

Mezzo-forte—(mf) Medium loud.

Mezzo-piano—(mp) Medium soft.

Minor—Less, when referring to intervals or scales. Opposed to major.

Moderato—A moderate, average tempo.

Modulation—The process of moving harmonically to a different key.

Round—A short song in two or more parts sung at different time intervals.

Rubato—Robbed time. Time taken from one note and given to another.

Scale—The succession of tones upon which music is built.

Score—The musical notation of a composition. The conductor's score.

Secular—Worldly, as opposed to religious.

Semitone—Half-tone.

Senza—Without.

Septet—A composition written for seven voices or instruments.

Serenade—A nocturnal love song.

Sextet—A composition written for six voices or instruments.

Sharp—A symbol (#) used to raise a tone one-half step in pitch.

Signature—A group of sharps or flats indicating the key of a composition. Figures indicating the meter of a composition.

Slur—Passing smoothly from one tone to another without break.

Solmization—The practice of applying syllable names to scale tones.

Solo—A composition for one voice or instrument.

Soprano—The highest female voice.

Sostenuto—Sustained.

Spiritual—A type of religious folksong peculiar to the American Negro.

Staccato—Detached; notes played sharply separated from each other. Indicated by dots (. . .) over notes.

Staff—The five parallel horizontal lines on which musical notes are written.

Stringendo—Faster.

Syncopate—To place the accent on an unconventional beat.

Tacet—Silent.

Tenor—The highest male voice.

Tenuto—Held. Sustained for full time value.

Tetrachord—A group of four notes, the basis of the Greek scale system.

Theme—A musical subject. Contrasted with *development*.

Tone—A musical sound of definite pitch.

Transposition—The process of performing in another than the written key.

Treble—The upper part; the highest voice.

Tremolo—A trembling or quivering. A shaking of the tone.

Triad—The common chord, consisting of a root, third, and fifth.

Tutti—All; used after a solo passage to mean all instruments or voices.

Unison—Two or more tones having the same pitch.

Vibrato—A tremulous effect, akin to tremolo but less marked.

Virtuoso—An accomplished artist.

Vivace—Lively, briskly.

Vivo—Animated, lively.

Monody—For one voice, as opposed to polyphony.

Morendo—Dying away; gradually diminishing the tone and the tempo.

Motet—A sacred choral composition, usually in contrapuntal style.

Natural—A symbol (♮) used to cancel the effect of a sharp or a flat.

Obbligato—An instrumental part usually accompanying a vocal solo.

Octet—A composition for eight voices or instruments.

Opera—A musical drama.

Opera comique—Comic opera.

Operetta—A light musical drama with spoken dialogue.

Oratorio—A sacred musical drama in concert form.

Overtones—Complementary harmonic sounds present in all musical tones.

Passion—A sacred composition depicting the suffering of Christ.

Pastorale—A musical picture of scenes from rural life.

Pentatonic—Five-tone.

Piano—(p) Soft. Also the ṗianoforte.

Pianissimo—(pp) Very soft.

Pitch—The rate of vibration of any given tone.

Piu—More.

Piu Mosso—More motion; quicker.

Plainsong—The name given to the earliest form of religious chant.

Poco a poco—Little by little.

Polyphonic—Many-voiced. Opposed to monophonic.

Prelude—Introductory movement of a composition. A musical form.

Prestissimo—As fast as possible.

Presto—Very fast.

Prima donna—A principal woman singer in opera.

Program (music)—Descriptive music. Opposed to absolute or pure music.

Quartet—A composition written for four voices or instruments.

Quintet—A composition written for five voices or instruments.

Rallentando—(rall.) Gradually slower.

Recitative—Musical declamation usually introducing an aria.

Recital—A form of musical program usually by one artist.

Repertory—A list of compositions which an artist has ready for performance.

Rhythm—A periodic recurrence of accent; regular pulsation.

Ritard—(rit.) Slower.

TABLE OF CONTENTS FOR CHORAL ARRANGEMENTS

Pledge Of Allegiance
Unison

LOIS RHEA

My House Of Life
Unison

Anon.

LOIS RH...

e-ven dies a glor-ious way.

rit. *slower*

The thresh-old be-neath my feet shall be hu-

mil - i - ty; The roof the ver - y sky it - self In-fin-i-

a tempo

ty. Give me wide walls to build my house, my house of life.

allarg. *ff*

rit. allarg. *ff*

He Shall Feed His Flock
(The "Messiah")
Unison

Isaiah XL: 11
Matthew Xi: 28, 29

GEORGE F. HANDE

He __ shall_ga - ther the lambs_with His arm, with _____ His arm,

cresc.

and car - ry__ them __ in His bo - som, and

mf *p*

gent-ly lead_ those_ that are __ with young,_ and gent-ly lead_ those,_ and

ten.

gent - ly lead_those,that are _with young.

ten.

ten. *mf* *p*

When I Was A Lad
(H. M. S. Pinafore)
Unison

WILLIAM S. GILBERT

ARTHUR S. SULLIVAN
Arr. by Lois Rhea

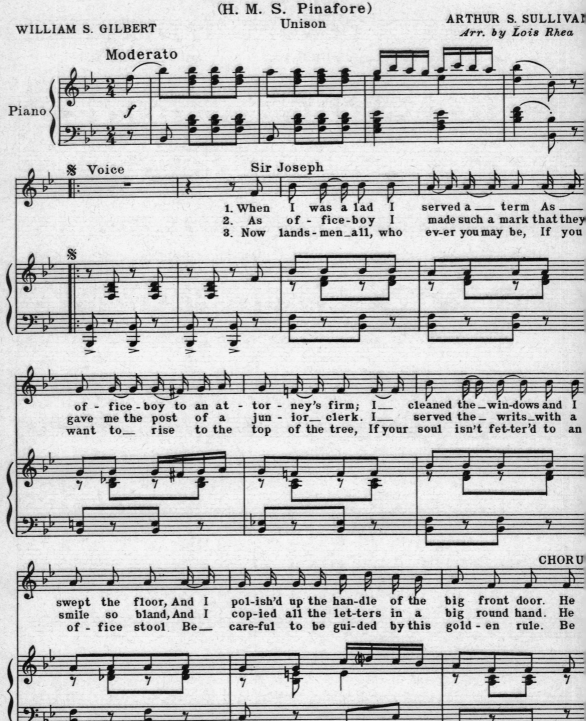

1. When I was a lad I served a ___ term As ___ of-fice-boy to an at-tor-ney's firm; I ___ cleaned the ___ win-dows and I swept the floor, And I pol-ish'd up the han-dle of the big front door. He

2. As of-fice-boy I made such a mark that they gave me the post of a jun-ior clerk. I ___ served the ___ writs ___ with a smile so bland, And I cop-ied all the let-ters in a big round hand. He

3. Now lands-men ___ all, who ev-er you may be, If you want to ___ rise to the top of the tree, If your soul isn't fet-ter'd to an of-fice stool Be ___ care-ful to be gui-ded by this gold-en rule. Be

Solo voice sings Sir Joseph part; Chorus sings chorus part (If chorus sings entire number, substitute I for He in sections marked Chorus)

Sir Joseph

pol - ish'd up the han - dle of the big front door. I
cop - ied all the let - ters in a big round hand. I
care - ful to be gui - ded by this gold - en rule. Stick

pol-ished up the han-dle so — care - ful - lee That — now I am the rul-er of the
cop-ied all the let-ters in a hand — so — free That — now I am the rul-er of the
close — to your desks, — and — nev-er go to sea, And you all — may be rul-ers of the

CHORUS

Queen's Na - vee! He pol-ished up the han-dle so — care - ful - lee That —
Queen's Na - vee! He cop - ied all the let-ters in a hand — so — free That —
Queen's Na - vee! Stick close — to your desks, — and — nev-er go to sea, And you

D. S. 𝄋 *(After third verse)*

now he is the rul - er of the Queen's Na - vee!
now he is the rul - er of the Queen's Na - vee!
all — may be rul - ers of the Queen's Na - vee!

D.S.

The Lord Is My Shepherd

(S. A. or T. B.)

KOSCHAT
Arr. by Lois Rhe

2780-140

e - vil I fear; _ Thy rod shall de - fend me, Thy staff be my

e - vil _ I _ fear; _ Thy rod _ shall _ de - fend _ me, Thy staff _ be my

stay; _ No harm can be - fall, with my Com-fort - er near; No

stay; _ No harm can _ be - fall, with my _ Com-fort - er near; No

harm can be - fall, with my Com - fort - er near. _____

harm _ can _ be - fall, with my _ Com - fort - er near. _____

The Glendy Burk
(S. A. or T. B.)

STEPHEN FOSTER
Arr. by Lois Rhea

1. Glen - dy Burk is a might-y fast boat, With a might-y fast cap - tain
2. Glen - dy Burk has a fun - ny old crew And they sing the boat - man's

1. Chug, chug, chug, chug, chug, chug, chug, chug, chug, chug,
2. Row, row, row, row, row, row, row, row, row, row,

too; He sits up there on the hur - ri - cane roof And he
song, They burn the pitch and the pine knot too, For to

chug, too - too. Chug, chug, chug, chug, chug, chug,
row, too - too. Row, row, row, row, row, row,

keeps his eye on the crew. I can't stay here, for they
shove the boat a - long. The smoke goes up and the

chug, chug, chug, chug, chug, too - too. I can't stay
row, row, row, row, row, too - too. The smoke goes

work too hard; I'm bound to leave this town; I'll take my duds and
in - gine roars And the wheel goes round and round, So fare you well! for I'll

here, I'm bound to leave town; I'll take my
up, The wheel goes round, round, So fare you

tote 'em on my back When the Glen - dy Burk comes down.
take a lit - tle ride When the Glen - dy Burk comes down.

duds, When the Glen - dy Burk comes down.
well, When the Glen - dy Burk comes down.

The Band Played On
(S. A. or T. B.)

CHARLES WARD
Arr. by Raymond Rhe

* Bass sings *8va lower*

Soprano or Tenor / Alto * or Bass / Piano

Cas- ey would waltz with a straw-ber- ry blonde, And the band played on, _____ He'll glide 'cross the floor with the girl he a - dor'd, And the band

Cas- ey would waltz with a straw-ber- ry blonde, And the band played, _ played _ on, He's glide 'cross the floor, And the

played on, _____ But his brain was so load-ed it near-ly ex-

band __ played on, _____ But his brain was load -

plod - ed, The poor girl would shake with a - larm, _____ He'd ne'er leave the

ed, _____ The poor girl would shake with a - larm, _____ He'd ne'er leave the

p

girl with the straw-ber-ry curl, And the band played on, _____ the

girl with the straw-ber-ry curl, And the band __ played on. _____

46

2780-140

on.   He_ near - ly ex - plod -

But his brain was so load - ed, it near - ly ex - plod - ed, The

ed, She shook with a - larm, _____ He would ne'er leave the

poor girl would shake with a - larm, _____ He'd ne'er leave the girl with the

rit.

girl _ be - hind, And the band played on _ and on.

rit.

straw - ber - ry curl, And the band played on. _____

rit.

Someone's In The Kitchen With Dinah

(S. A. or T. B.)

Arr. by Lois Rhea

Over The River

(S. A. or T. B.)
(With Opt. Descant)

Traditional
Arr. by Lois Rhea

2780-140   Made in U. S. A.

SOPRANO or TENOR
2. O - ver the riv - er and thro' the wood   to have   a first - rate

ALTO or BASS
2. O - ver the riv - er and thro' the wood   to have   a first - rate

DESCANT (opt.)
2. O -   ver   the riv -   er   to have   a

play;___   Oh,   hear the bells ring,   "ting - a - ling - ling!" Hur

play;___   Oh,   hear the bells ring,   "ting - a - ling - ling!" Hur

play;___   Hear   the   bells_ ring, "ting   -   ling!"

(*Christmas* may replace
Thanksgiving: if desired)

rah for Thanks-giv - ing   Day!_   O-ver the riv-er and thro' the wood, Tro

rah for Thanks-giv - ing   Day!_   O-ver the riv-er and thro' the wood, Tro

Thanks   -   giv - ing   Day!_   O -   ver   the riv -   er,   Tro

780-140

Long, Long Ago

S. S. A.
for Christmas

Anonymous

LOIS RHE.

56

Sing-ing their songs of joy,___ Long, long a-go.

Sing-ing their songs of joy,___ Long, long a-go.

Sing-ing their songs of joy,___ Long a-go.

Meno mosso

For in a man-ger bed,___ Cra-dled in love, we know.___

For in a man-ger bed,___ Cra-dled in love, we know.___

For in a man-ger bed, a bed, Cra-dled in love,___ we know.

Molto rit.

Solo or a few Sopranos

Christ came to Beth-le-hem___ Long, long a-go.___

Christ came to Beth-le-hem___ Long, long a-go.

Christ came to Beth-le-hem___ Long,_long a-go.

2780-140

Some Day My Prince Will Come

From "Snow White and the Seven Dwarfs"
S. S. A.

LARRY MOREY

FRANK CHURCHILL
Arr. by Lois Rhea

780-140

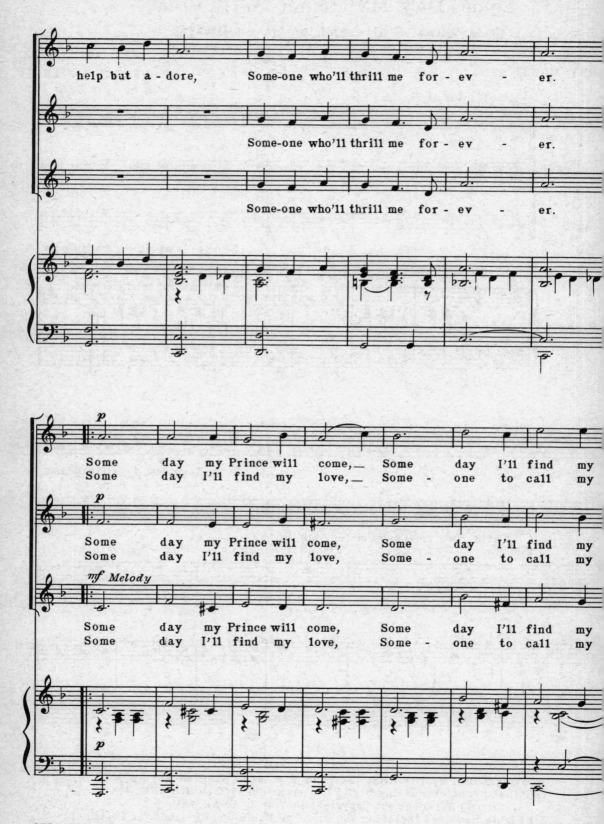

help but a - dore, Some-one who'll thrill me for - ev - er.

Some-one who'll thrill me for - ev - er.

Some-one who'll thrill me for - ev - er.

Some day my Prince will come,— Some day I'll find my
Some day I'll find my love,— Some - one to call my

Some day my Prince will come, Some day I'll find my
Some day I'll find my love, Some - one to call my

mf Melody

Some day my Prince will come, Some day I'll find my
Some day I'll find my love, Some - one to call my

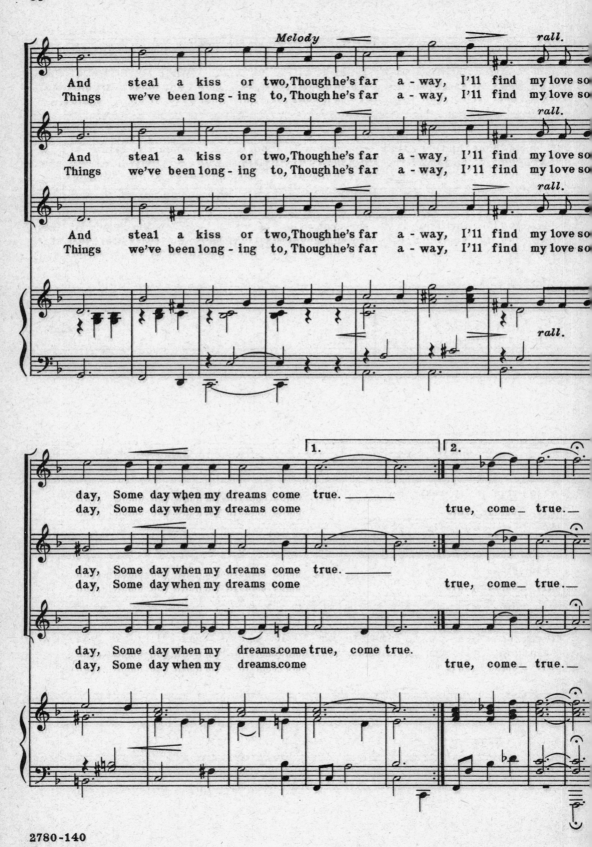

On Wings Of Song

S. S. A.

ree translation by R. R.

FELIX MENDELSSOHN
Arr. by Raymond Rhea

62

2780-140

wait - ing To wel-come thy moonbeams there.
Gan - ges Re-mind where its wa-ters lie.

wait - ing To wel-come thy moonbeams there.
Gan - ges Re-mind where its wa-ters lie.

wait - ing To wel-come thy moonbeams there.
Gan - ges Re-mind where its wa-ters lie.

1.

2. Each

2. Each

2. Each

2.

Out un-der the spread-ing palm trees, Where

Out un-der the spread-ing palm trees, Where

Out un-der the spread-ing palm trees, Where

rays of moon - light gleam, _____ Our hearts shall fill _ with

rays of moon - light gleam, _____ Our hearts shall fill with

rays of moon - light gleam, _____ Our hearts shall fill with

rap - ture As once a-gain _ we dream, _____ as

rap - ture As once a-gain we dream, _____ as

rap - ture As once a-gain we dream, _____ as

once a - gain _____ we dream. _____

once a - gain _____ we dream. _____

once a - gain _____ we dream. _____

Lavender's Blue
S. S. A.

Traditional

English Folk Song
Arr. by Raymond Rhe

Soprano I: Dil - ly, dil - ly, dil - ly, lav - en - der's blue.___

Soprano II: Dil - ly, dil - ly, dil - ly, lav - en - der's blue.___

Alto: Dil - ly, dil - ly, dil - ly, lav - en - der's blue.___

Piano — *mf (For rehearsal)*

Ah ___ Lav - en-der's green, Ah ___

Ah ___ Lav - en-der's green, Ah ___

Lav - en-der's blue, dil-ly, dil-ly, Lav - en - der's green, When I am King, dil-ly, dil-ly,

some with a fork;— Some to make hay, dil-ly dil-ly, some to thresh corn,

some with a fork;— Some to make hay, dil - ly, some to thresh corn,

some with a fork;— Some to make hay, dil - ly, some to thresh corn,

While you and I, dil-ly, dil-ly, keep our-selves warm. Lav-en-der's blue, dil-ly, dil-ly,

While you and_I, dil - ly, keep our-selves warm. Lav-en-der's blue, dil-ly, dil-ly,

While you and_I, dil - ly, keep our-selves warm. Lav-en-der's blue, dil-ly, dil-ly,

rit.   *a tempo*   *Melody*

lav - en - der's green. If it should hap, dil-ly, dil-ly, if it should chance,

rit.   *a tempo*

lav - en - der's green. If it should hap, dil-ly, dil-ly, if it should chance,

rit.   *a tempo*   *Melody*

lav - en - der's green. If it should hap, dil-ly, dil-ly, if it should chance,

rit.   *a tempo*

Bobo The Bass
T. T. B.

R. R.

RAYMOND RHE

2780-140

72

2780-140

squeak had left, Their voi-ces both did fail. A task such he-roes

squeak had left, Their voi-ces both did fail. A task such he-roes

squeak had left, Their voi-ces both did fail. A task such he-roes

it would be to find on land or foam; A champ the peo-ple

it would be to find on land or foam; A champ the peo-ple

it would be to find on land or foam; A champ the peo-ple

were to choose, But they had all gone home!

were to choose, But they had all gone home!

were to choose, But they had all gone home!

My Heart's In The Highlands

T. T. B.

ROBERT BURNS   RAYMOND RHEA

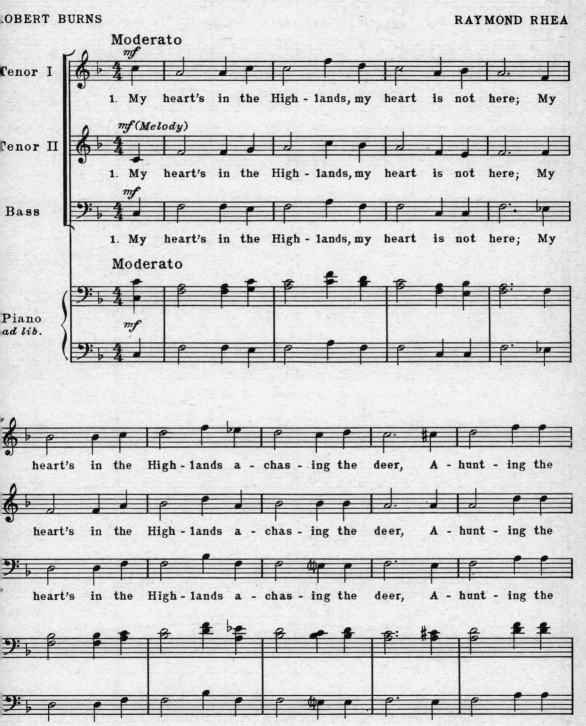

2780-140

76

2780-140

ev - er I wan - der, wher ev - er I rove, The hills of the

ev - er I wan - der, wher ev - er I rove, The hills of the

ev - er I wan - der, wher ev - er I rove, The hills of the

high - lands for - ev - er I love.   3. Fare - well to the moun - tains, high -
                          4. My heart's in the High - lands, my

high - lands for - ev - er I love.   3. Fare - well to the moun - tains, high -
                          4. My heart's in the High - lands, my

high - lands for - ev - er I love.   3. Fare - well to the moun - tains, high -
                          4. My heart's in the High - lands, my

cov - er'd with snow; Fare - well to the straths and green val - leys be -
heart is not here; My heart's in the High - lands a - chas - ing the

cov - er'd with snow; Fare - well to the straths and green val - leys be -
heart is not here; My heart's in the High - lands a - chas - ing the

cov - er'd with snow; Fare - well to the straths and green val - leys be -
heart is not here; My heart's in the High - lands a - chas - ing the

78

2780-140

Haul Away, Joe

T. T. B.

Chantey
Arr. by Raymond Rhea

2780-140

haul a-way, Joe.__ A-way, haul a-way,__ come rock and roll me

haul a-way, Joe.__ A-way, haul a-way,__ come rock and roll me

haul a-way, Joe.__ A-way, haul a-way,__ come rock and roll me

o - ver, A-way, haul a-way,__ haul a-way, Joe.__

o - ver, A-way, haul a-way,__ haul a-way, Joe.__

o - ver, A-way, haul a-way,__ haul a-way, Joe.__

D.S. ⊕ CODA
rit.

Haul a-way, haul a-way, haul a-way, Joe.__ Haul a-way,__ Joe.__

rit.

Haul a-way, haul a-way, haul a-way, Joe.__ Haul a-way, Joe.__

rit.

Haul a-way, haul a-way, haul a-way, Joe.__ A-Haul a-way,__ Joe.__

CODA

D.S. ⊕
rit.

Ev'ry Time I Feel The Spirit

TTB

Spiritual
Arr. by Raymond Rho

Whistle While You Work

From "Snow White and the Seven Dwarfs"
S-A-Cambiata-Baritone

LARRY MOREY

FRANK CHURCHILL
Arr. by Raymond Rhe

fel - low needs a song._____ Doc - tor, Bank - er,

_____ a song.____ Doc - tor, Bank - er,

_____ a song.____ Whis - tle while you

_____ a song.____ Whis - tle while you

Butch - er, Bak - er, You can be a mer - ry mak - er, If you'll keep on

Butch - er, Bak - er, You can be a mer - ry mak - er, Ah,_____

work, Whis - tle while you work, Ah,_____

work, Whis - tle while you work, Ah,_____

sing-ing all day long.

If you're hang-ing in sus-pense fro

And you want to keep the sense of hu-mor a - live.

eight 'til five,

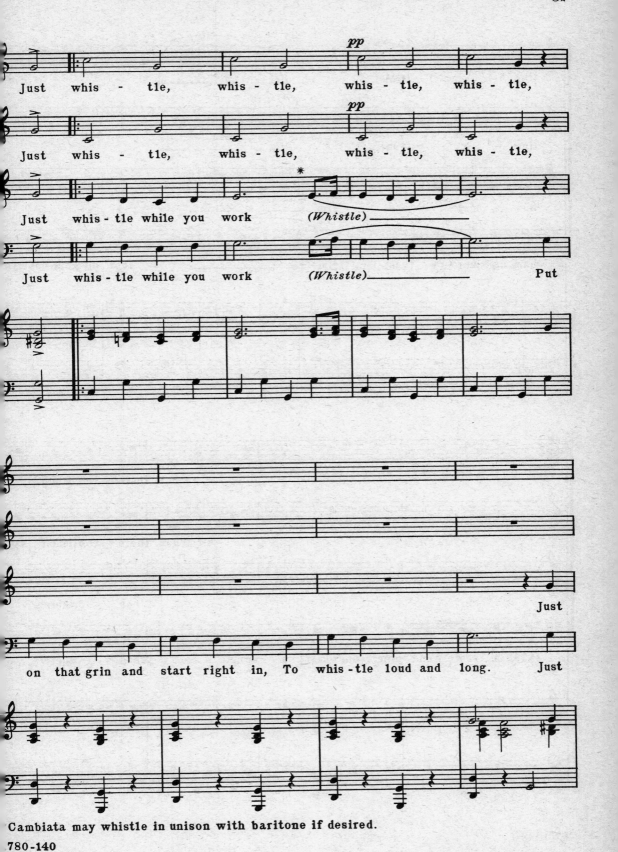

Just whis - tle, whis - tle, whis - tle, whis - tle,

Just whis - tle, whis - tle, whis - tle, whis - tle,

Just whis - tle while you work *(Whistle)*

Just whis - tle while you work *(Whistle)* Put

Just

on that grin and start right in, To whis - tle loud and long. Just

Cambiata may whistle in unison with baritone if desired.

Hum a tune. Hm. hum a merry tune. Hm. hum a merry tune. Hm. Just do your best, Th

When there's too much to When there's too much to When there's take a rest, And sing your-self a song. When there's

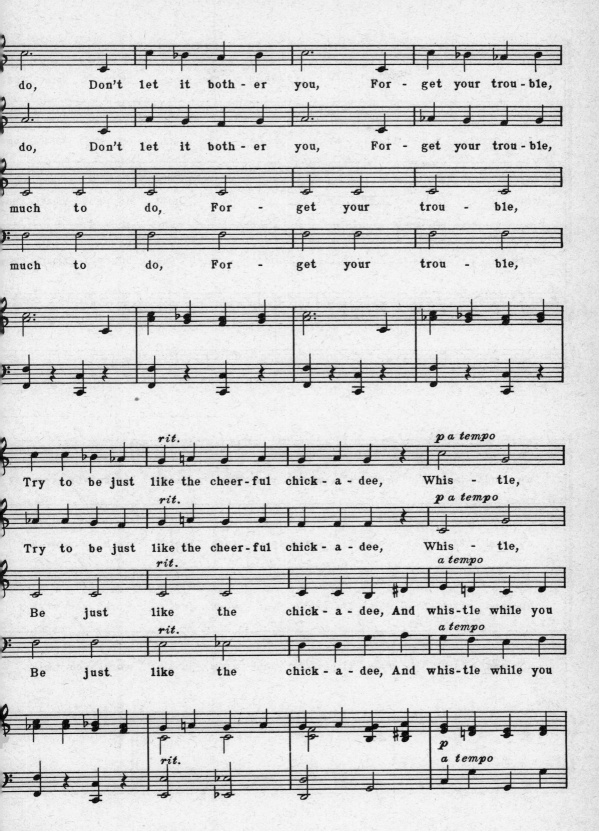

do,   Don't let   it   both - er   you,   For - get your trou - ble,

do,   Don't let   it   both - er   you,   For - get your trou - ble,

much   to   do,   For -   get   your   trou - ble,

much   to   do,   For -   get   your   trou - ble,

rit.   *p a tempo*

Try to be just like the cheer - ful chick - a - dee,   Whis - tle,

rit.   *p a tempo*

Try to be just like the cheer - ful chick - a - dee,   Whis - tle,

rit.   *a tempo*

Be   just   like   the   chick - a - dee, And whis-tle while you

rit.   *a tempo*

Be   just   like   the   chick - a - dee, And whis-tle while you

rit.   *a tempo*

When You Wish Upon A Star
"Pinocchio"
S-A-Cambiata-Baritone

NED WASHINGTON

LEIGH HARLINE
Arr. by Raymond Rhea

780-140

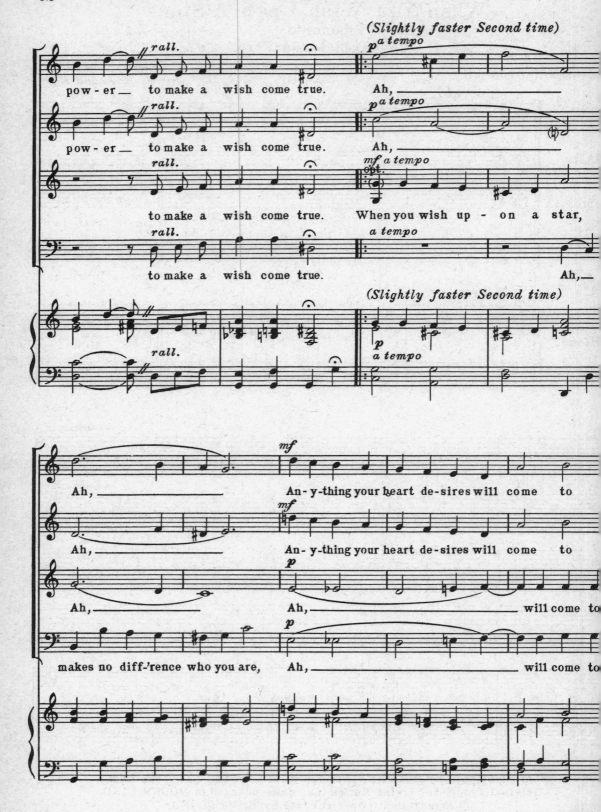

you.   Ah, ———————   Ah, ———————

you.   Ah, ———————   Ah, ———————

you, to you.   If your heart is   in your dream,   Ah, ———————

you, to you.—   Ah,—   no re-quest is   too ex-treme,

When you wish up - on a star as dream - ers   do.

When you wish up - on a star as dream - ers,   dream - ers do.—

Ah, ———————————————   as dream-ers, dream-ers do.—

Ah, ———————————————   as dream-ers do.

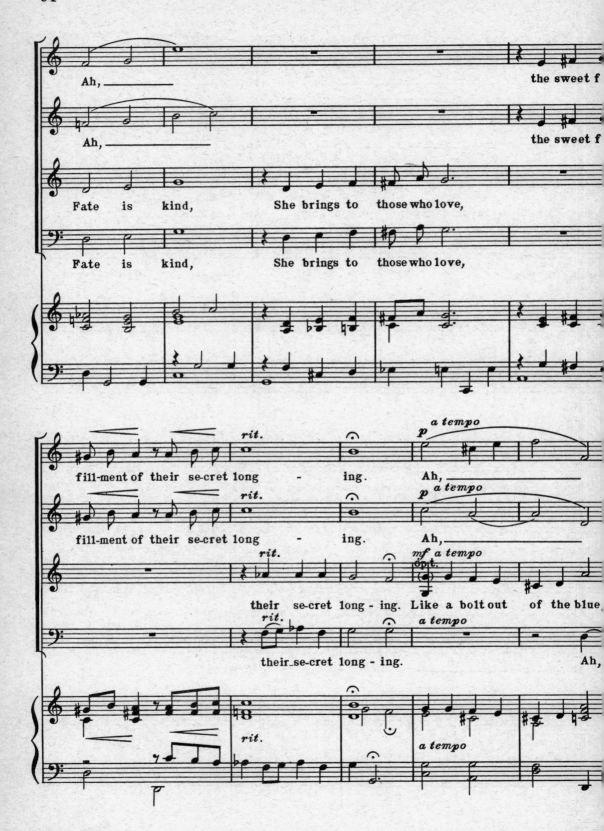

Ah, _____ When you wish up - on a star your

Ah, _____ When you wish up - on a star your

Ah, _____ Ah, _____

Fate steps in and sees you through, Ah, _____

1. dream comes true. **2.** dream comes true. _____

dream comes true. dream, your dream comes true. _____

_____ your dream comes true. _____ your dream comes true. _____

_____ your dream comes true. _____ your dream comes true. _____

1. **2.**

Heigh Ho
The Dwarfs' Marching Song
From "Snow White and the Seven Dwarfs"
For Cambiata and Baritone

LARRY MOREY

FRANK CHURCHILL
Arr. by Lois Rhea

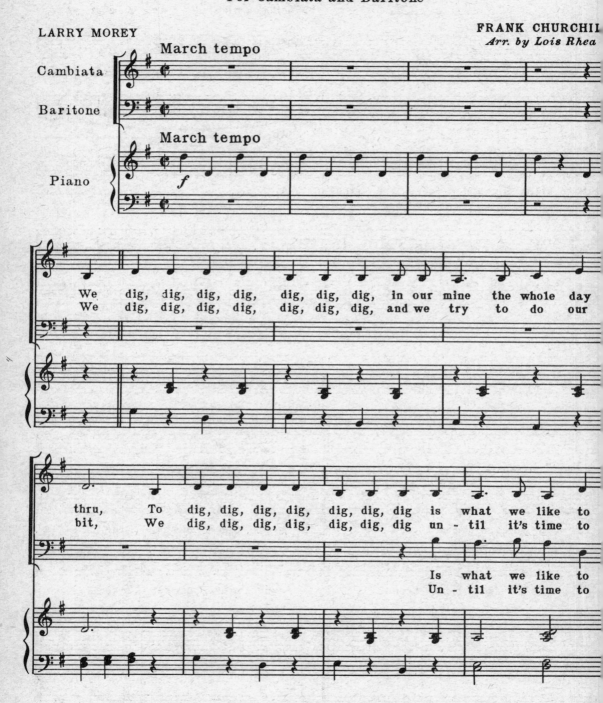

Cambiata

Baritone

March tempo

Piano

March tempo

We dig, dig, dig, dig, dig, dig, dig, in our mine the whole day
We dig, dig, dig, dig, dig, dig, dig, and we try to do our

thru, To dig, dig, dig, dig, dig, dig, dig is what we like to
bit, We dig, dig, dig, dig, dig, dig, dig un-til it's time to

Is what we like to
Un-til it's time to

2780-140

do.
quit.

do.   And while we dig, we al - ways sing, For _ when you dig there
quit.   And then we war - ble down the scale, As we all go march - ing

You can whis - tle
To the rhy - thm

ain't a bet-ter thing than a tune,   Than a tune,
down _ the _ trail right a - long,   Right a - long,

or   can   croon. _____
of   the   song. _____

(Whistle)

"Heigh - Ho,"   "Heigh -

98

2780-140

can't go wrong With a "Heigh" "Heigh - Ho,"

(Whistle) "Heigh - Ho," "Heigh-

Ho," "Heigh Ho," It's home from work we go, Just

"Heigh Ho," "Heigh Ho," It's home from work we go, (Whistle)

keep on sing - ing all day long "Heigh - Ho,"

"Heigh - Ho," "Heigh-

100

"Heigh-Ho," "Heigh - Ho," "Heigh - Ho," All sev - en in a

Ho," "Heigh-Ho," "Heigh-Ho," All sev - en in a

row, You pos - i - tive - ly can't go wrong

row, (Whistle) With a

With a "Heigh," "Heigh - Ho," "Heigh - Ho."

"Heigh," "Heigh - Ho," "Heigh - Ho."

Beautiful Savior

S. A. B.

12th Century
Arr. by Lois Rhea

1. Beau - ti - ful Sav - ior, Lord of all na - ture, O Thou of God and_ man the Son, Thee will I cher - ish,
2. Fair are the mea - dows, Fair - er the wood-lands, Robed in_ bloom - ing_ garb of spring; Je - sus is fair - er,

30-140

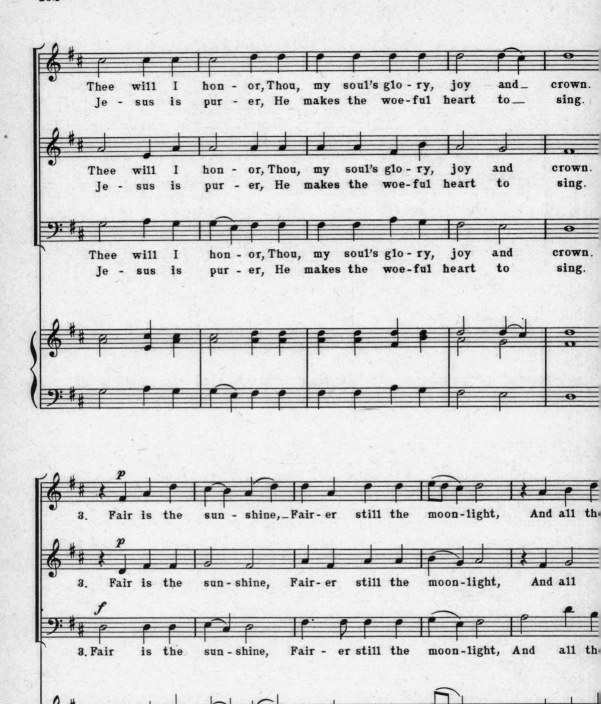

twink - ling __ star - ry __ host; __ Je - sus shines bright - er, __

twink - ling __ star - ry host; Je - sus shines bright-er,

twink - ling __ star - ry host; Je - sus shines bright-er,

rit. *ff*

Je - sus shines pur - er Than all the an-gels heav'n can __ boast.

rit. *ff*

Je - sus shines pur - er Than all the an-gels heav'n can __ boast. __

rit. *ff*

Je - sus shines pur - er Than all the an-gels heav'n can boast.

rit. *ff*

Ode To The Nation

S. A. B.

From Ninth Sympho...
BEETHOVEN
Arr. by Raymond Rh...

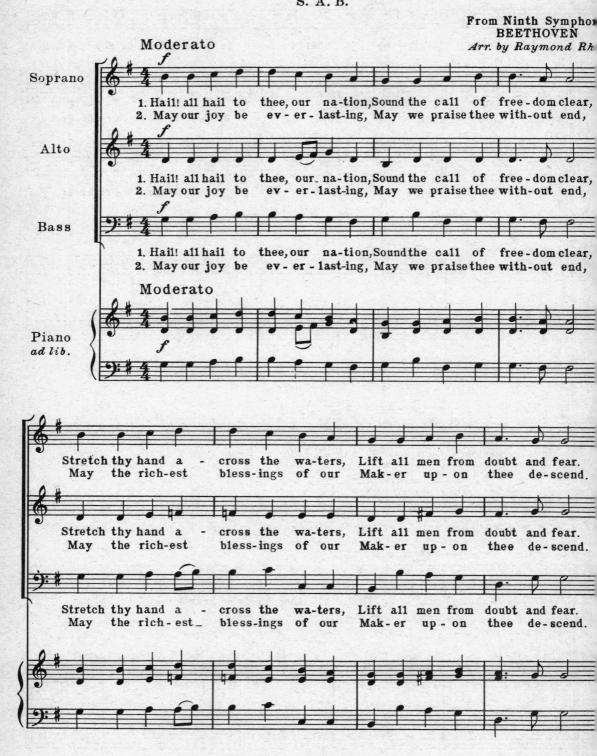

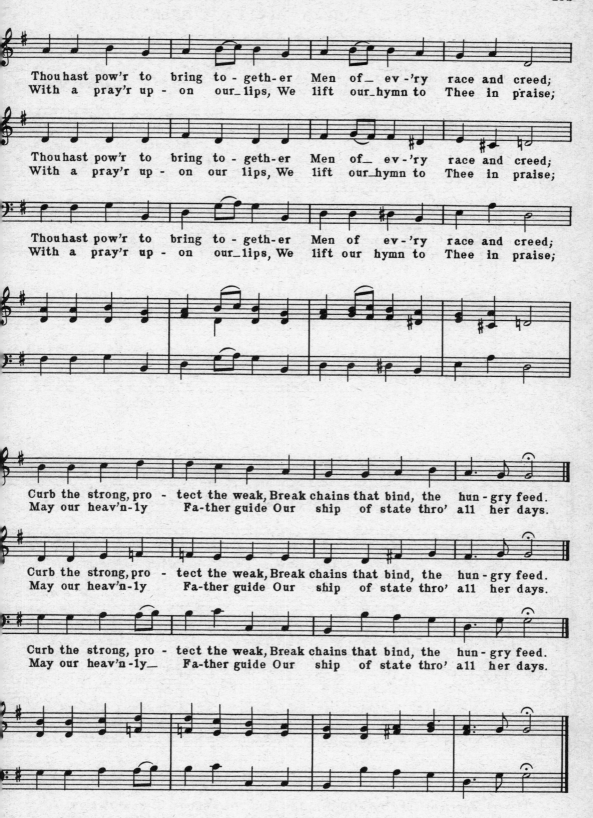

Thou hast pow'r to bring to - geth-er Men of_ ev -'ry race and creed;
With a pray'r up - on our_ lips, We lift our_ hymn to Thee in praise;

Thou hast pow'r to bring to - geth-er Men of_ ev -'ry race and creed;
With a pray'r up - on our lips, We lift our_ hymn to Thee in praise;

Thou hast pow'r to bring to - geth-er Men of ev -'ry race and creed;
With a pray'r up - on our_ lips, We lift our hymn to Thee in praise;

Curb the strong, pro - tect the weak, Break chains that bind, the hun - gry feed.
May our heav'n-ly Fa-ther guide Our ship of state thro' all her days.

Curb the strong, pro - tect the weak, Break chains that bind, the hun - gry feed.
May our heav'n-ly Fa-ther guide Our ship of state thro' all her days.

Curb the strong, pro - tect the weak, Break chains that bind, the hun - gry feed.
May our heav'n-ly_ Fa-ther guide Our ship of state thro' all her days.

We Wish You A Merry Christmas

S. A. B.

English Folk Song
Arr. by Lois Rhe...

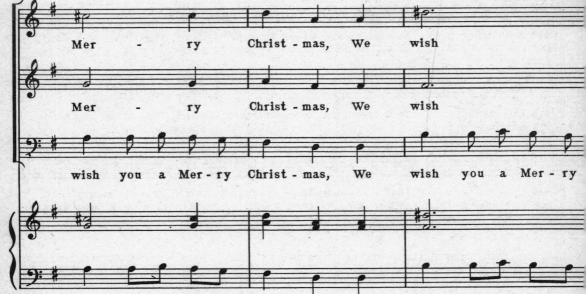

108

wish you a Mer - ry

wish you a Mer - ry

wish you a Mer - ry Christ - mas, We wish you a Mer - ry

Christ - mas, We wish you ___ a

Christ - mas, We wish you ___ a

Christ - mas, We wish you a Mer - ry Christ - mas, And a

Hap - py New Year! And a Hap - py New Year.

Hap - py New Year! And Hap - py New ___ Year.

Hap - py New Year! And Hap - py New Year.

Ring, Ring The Banjo

S. A. B.

STEPHEN FOSTER
Arr. by Lois Rhea

1. The time is nev - er drear - y,   If we
2. O come a - gain my dar - ling, By the
3. Oh nev - er count the bub - bles, When there's

nev - er, nev - er groans, The la - dies nev - er wea - ry, With the
gas - light of the moon, We'll turn the old pi - an - o, When the
wa - ter in the spring A fel - low has no trou - bles, While he's

Gloria Patri

S. A. B.

PALESTRINA
Arr. by Raymond Rhea

112

2780-140

As I Sat Under A Sycamore Tree

S. A. B.
Christmas

Traditional

Arr. by Lois Rhea

114

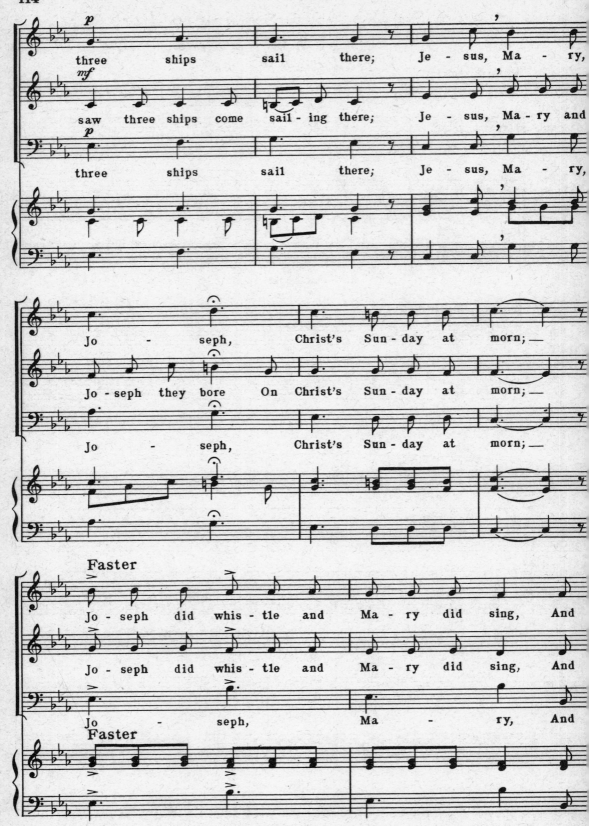

2780-140

all_ the bells_ on earth_ did ring_ For joy our Lord_was

bells on earth ring, Our Lord was

bells on earth ring, Our Lord was

born.____ Hm

born.____ Hm

born.____ O they sailed in - to Beth - le - hem, Saint

Slower

Mi - chael was_ the steers_ man, Saint John sat in the

116

2780-140

The Ash-Grove

S. A. B.

JOHN OXENFORD

Welsh Folk Song
Arr. by Lois Rhea

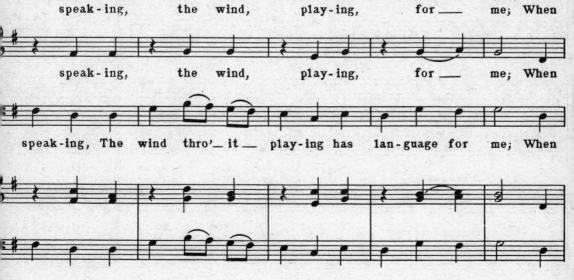

Soprano: Ash - grove, grace - ful, plain - ly,

Alto: Ash - grove, grace - ful, plain - ly,

Bass (mf Melody): The ash - grove, how — grace - ful, how plain - ly — 'tis —

Soprano: speak - ing, the wind, play - ing, for — me; When

Alto: speak - ing, the wind, play - ing, for — me; When

Bass: speak - ing, The wind thro'— it — play - ing has lan - guage for me; When

30-140

118

over its branch-es the sun-light is break-ing, A host of kind

over its branch-es the sun-light is break-ing, A host of kind

over its branch-es the sun-light is break-ing, A host of kind

fa-ces is gaz-ing on me. Friends of child-hood

fa-ces is gaz-ing on me. Friends of child-hood

fa-ces is gaz-ing on me, the friends a-

are be-fore me, Fond mem-o-ries wak-en as free-ly I

are be-fore me, Fond mem-o-ries wak-en as free-ly I

gain. Fond mem-o-ries wak-en as free-ly I

searching the leafy green dome, I find other faces fond

searching the leafy green dome, I find other faces fond

searching the leafy green dome, I find other faces fond

bending to greet me: The ash-grove, the ash-grove a-

bending to greet me: The ash-grove, the ash-grove a-

bending to greet me: The ash-grove, the ash-grove a-

lone is my home, The ash-grove my home.

lone is my home, The ash-grove my home.

lone is my home, The ash-grove my home.

rit.

I Ain't Gonna Grieve My Lord No More

S. A. B.

Spiritual
Arr. by Lois Rhea

And say a pray'r! Oh, you can't get to heav'n in a rock-ing chair, Get down on your
The pear-ly gates. Oh, you can't get to heav'n on rol-ler skates, You'll roll right
And pull me through. Oh, if you get there be-fore I do, Just bore a

And say a pray'r! Oh, you can't get to heav'n in a rock-ing chair, Get down on your
The pear-ly gates. Oh, you can't get to heav'n on rol-ler skates, You'll roll right
And pull me through. Oh, if you get there be-fore I do, Just bore a

pray'r! _____ Oh, you can't get to heav'n in a rock-ing chair, Get down on your
gates. _____ Oh, you can't get to heav'n on rol-ler skates, You'll roll right
through. _____ Oh, if you get there be-fore I do, Just bore a

f - first time
pp - repeat

knees and say a pray'r,
by the pear-ly gates, I ain't gon-na grieve my Lord no more. I ain't gon-na
hole and pull me through.

f - first time
pp - repeat

knees and say a pray'r,
by the pear-ly gates, I ain't gon-na grieve my Lord no more. I ain't gon-na
hole and pull me through.

f - first time
pp - repeat

knees and say a pray'r,
by the pear-ly gates, I ain't gon-na grieve my Lord no more. I ain't gon-na
hole and pull me through.

f - first time
pp - repeat

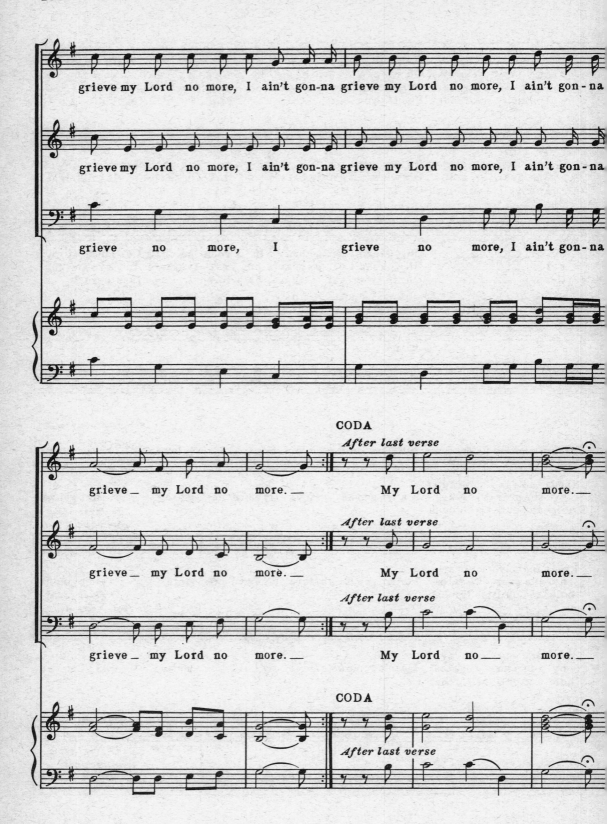

All Things Are Thine

S. A. T. B.

st verse _ J. G. Whittier
nd verse _ R. Rhea

J. S. BACH

2780-140

Pastorale
S. A. T. B.

RAYMOND RHEA

Hm _____ Hm _____

Hm _____ Hm _____

Hm _____ Hm _____

Hm _____ Hm _____

Hm _____

Hm _____

Hm _____

Hm _____

128

2780-140

Now Thank We All Our God

S. A. T. B.

MARTIN RINKART

. by Catherine Winkworth

J. S. BACH

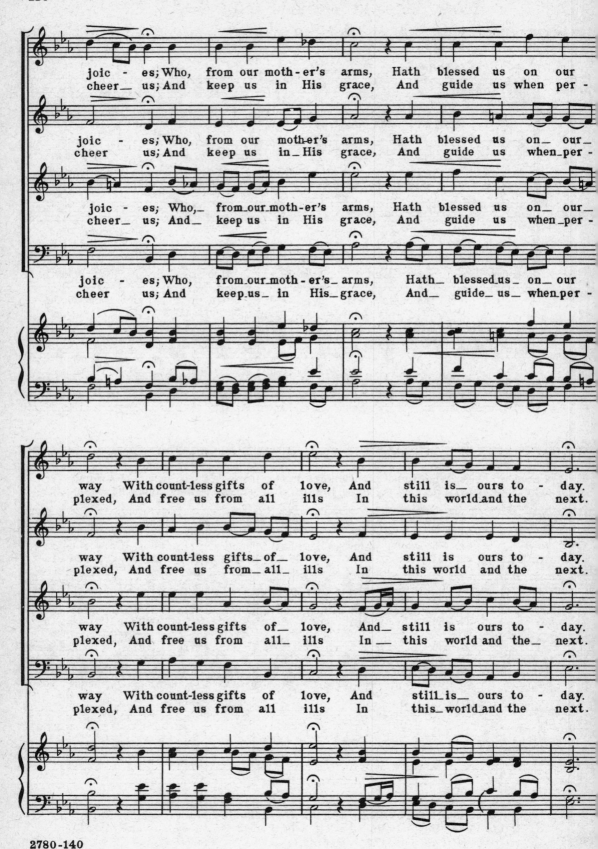

joic - es; Who, from our moth-er's arms, Hath blessed us on our
cheer_ us; And keep us in His grace, And guide us when per -

way With count-less gifts of love, And still is_ ours to - day.
plexed, And free us from all ills In this world and the next.

American Potpourri

S. A. T. B.

Arr. by Raymond Rhea

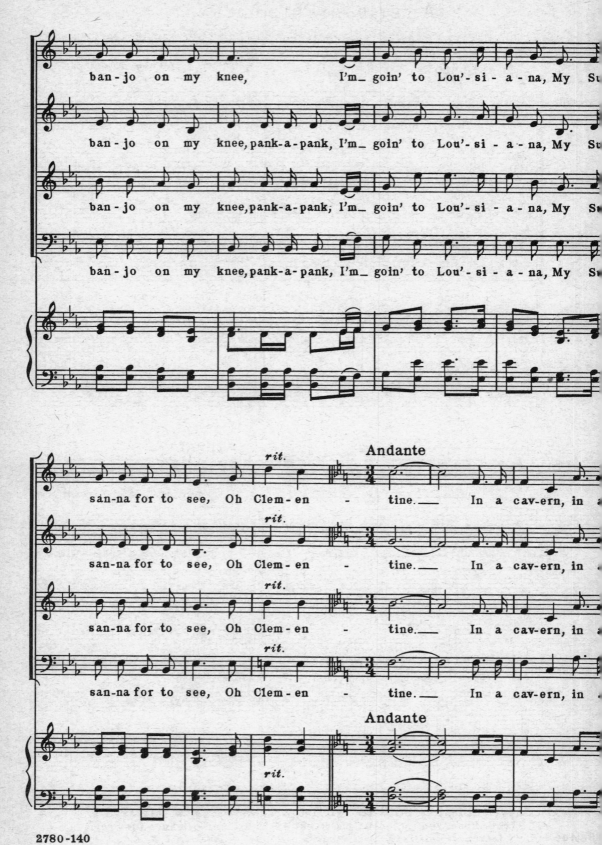

ban-jo on my knee, I'm goin' to Lou'-si-a-na, My Su

ban-jo on my knee, pank-a-pank, I'm goin' to Lou'-si-a-na, My Su

ban-jo on my knee, pank-a-pank, I'm goin' to Lou'-si-a-na, My Su

ban-jo on my knee, pank-a-pank, I'm goin' to Lou'-si-a-na, My Su

rit. **Andante**

san-na for to see, Oh Clem-en - tine.__ In a cav-ern, in a

san-na for to see, Oh Clem-en - tine.__ In a cav-ern, in a

san-na for to see, Oh Clem-en - tine.__ In a cav-ern, in a

san-na for to see, Oh Clem-en - tine.__ In a cav-ern, in a

Andante

rit.

rit.

rit.

rit.

can - yon, Ex-ca - vat - ing for a mine, Dwelt a min - er, for - ty

can - yon, Ex-ca - vat - ing for a mine, Dwelt a min - er, for - ty

can - yon, Ex-ca - vat - ing for a mine, Dwelt a min - er, for - ty

can - yon, Ex-ca - vat - ing for a mine, Dwelt a min - er, for - ty

nin - er and his daugh-ter Clem-en - tine.   Clem-en-tine,

nin - er and his daugh-ter Clem-en - tine.   Clem-en-tine,

nin - er and his daugh-ter Clem-en - tine.   Clem-en-tine,

nin - er and his daugh-ter Clem-en - tine. Oh my dar - ling, Oh my

134

2780-140

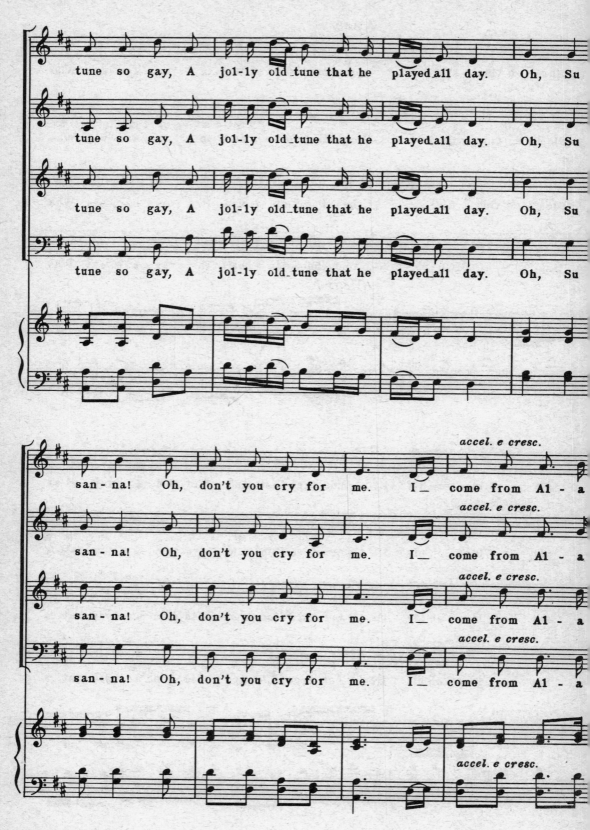

The Land We Love Is Calling

S.A.T.B.

Anon.

RAYMOND RHEA

light. _____ From coast to coast the an - swer Comes
light, _____ Join hands a - cross the na - tion From

ring - ing strong and free: A - mer - i - ca, A - mer - i - ca, We
toss - ing sea to sea; O God, may our A - mer - i - ca Bring

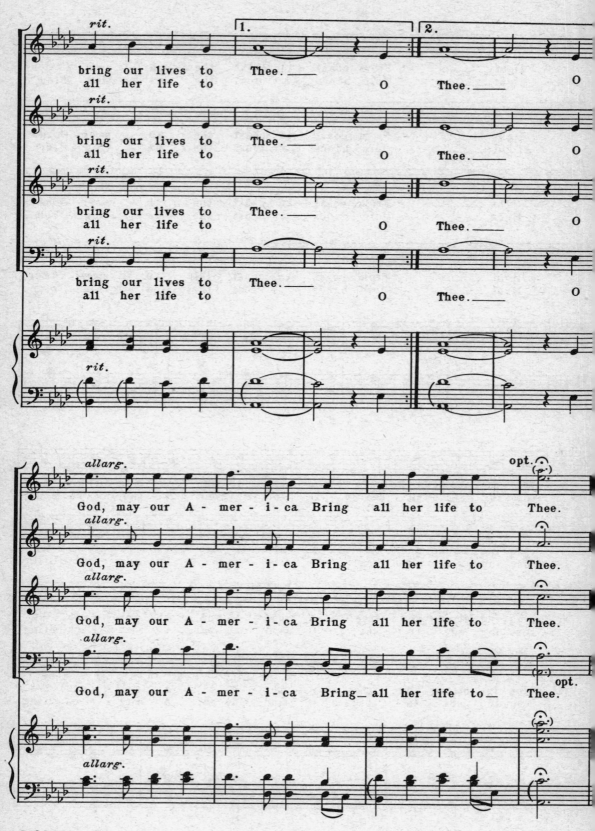

Bonnie Doon
S.A.T.B.

ROBERT BURNS

Old Scotch Air
Arr. by Raymond Rhea

Ye banks and braes o' bon-nie Doon, How can_ ye bloom_sae
Oft hae I rov'd_by bon-nie Doon, To see_ the rose_and

fresh_ and fair? How can ye chaunt, ye lit-tle birds,_And
wood-bine twine; When il-ka bird_ sang o'_ its love,_And

142

2780-140

Come With Me

S.A.T.B.

Italian Melody
Arr. by Raymond Rhe[a]

B.S. BARCLAY

146

2780 -140

Break Forth, O Beauteous Heavenly Light

S.A.T.B.

J. S. BACH
Arr. by Raymond Rhea

2780-140

148

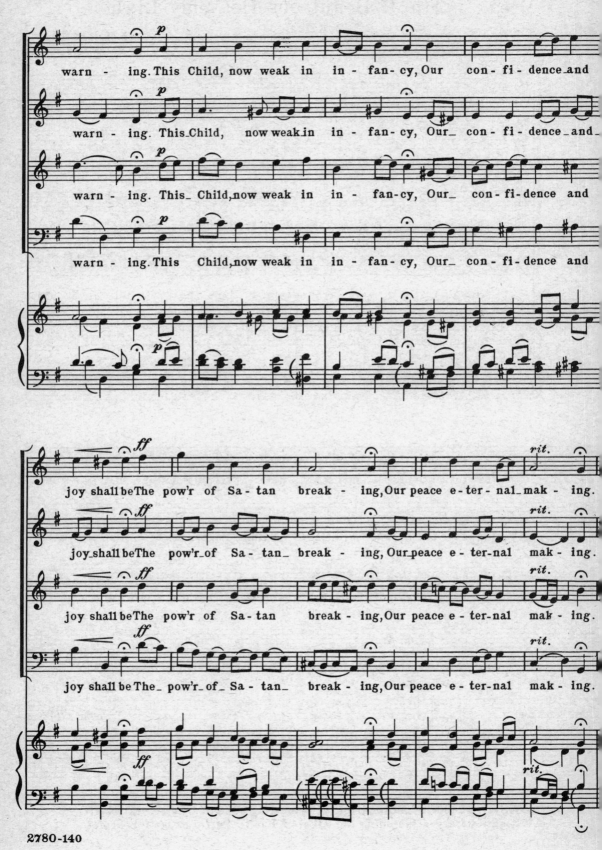

2780-140

O Bone Jesu
(O Precious Savior)
S.A.T.B.

translated by R.R.

GIOVANNI P. da PALESTRINA
Ed. by Raymond Rhea

80-140

150

2780-140

Hunting Song

S. A. T. B.

Sir WALTER SCOTT

RAYMOND RHEA

2780-140   *International Copyright Secured*   *Made in U. S. A.*

dawns the day, All the jol-ly chase is here With hawk and horse and
dawns the day, All the jol-ly chase is here With hawk and horse and
dawns the day, All the jol-ly chase is here With hawk and horse and
dawns the day, All the jol-ly chase is here With hawk and horse and

hunt - ing spear; Tan-ta-ra! Tan-ta-ra!
hunt - ing spear; Tan-ta-ra! Tan-ta-ra!
hunt - ing spear; Hounds are in their cou - ples yell - ing,
hunt - ing spear;

154

2780-140

156

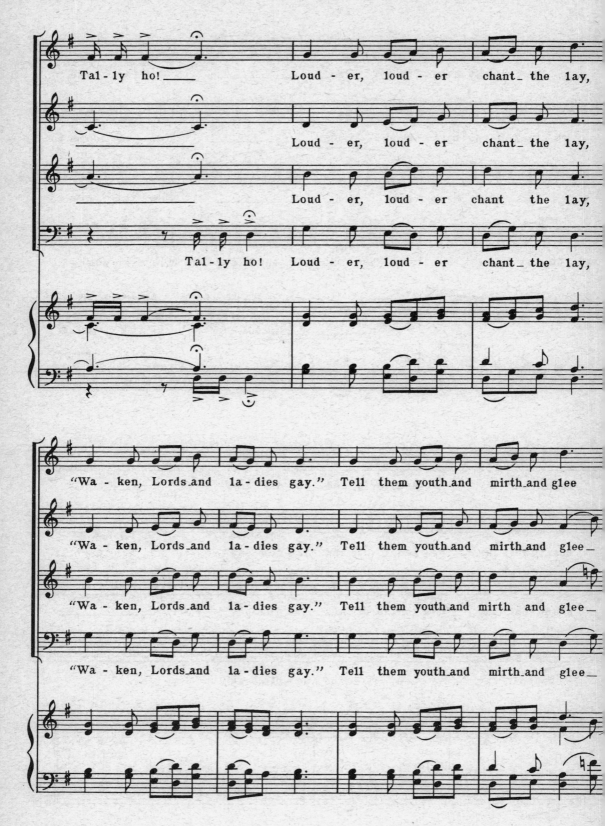

2780-140

rise with the day, Gen-tle lords and la - dies gay!___ Tal-ly-

rise with the day, Gen-tle lords and la - dies gay!___

rise with the day, Gen-tle lords and la - dies gay!___

rise with the day, Gen-tle lords and la - dies gay!___

ho!_____ Tal-ly ho!___

Tal-ly ho!_____ Tal-ly ho!___

Tal-ly ho!_____ Tal-ly ho!___

Tal-ly ho!_____ Tal-ly ho!___

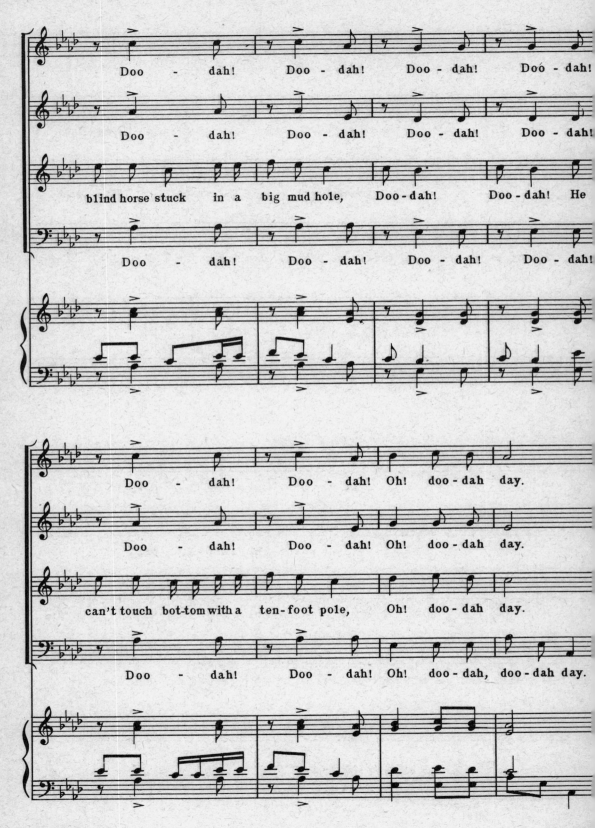

780-140

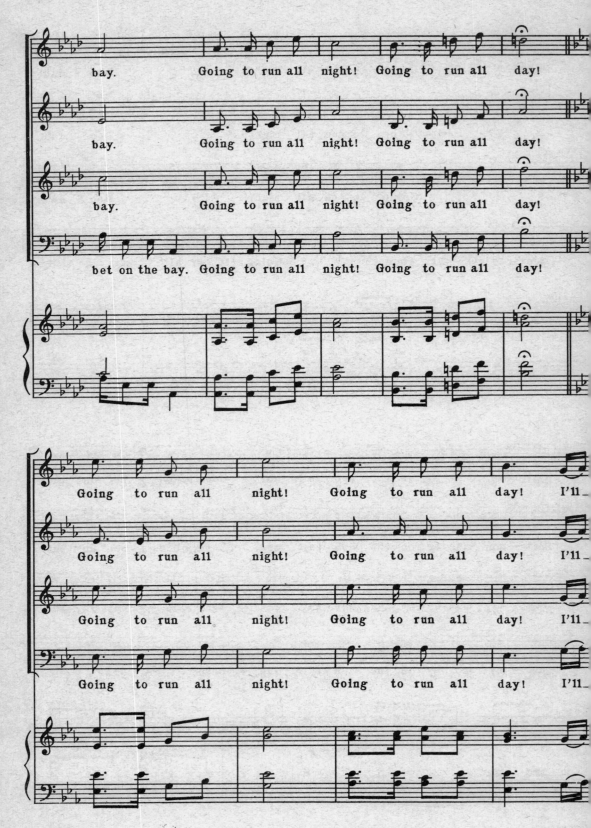